Vic Widman's

TRAVELLING THE
OUTBACK

BOILING BILLY
PUBLICATIONS

www.boilingbilly.com.au

WOODSLANE

www.woodslane.com.au

Boiling Billy, a licensed imprint of
Woodslane Press Pty Ltd
Unit 7/5 Vuko Place
Warriewood NSW 2102 Australia
Email: info@woodslane.com.au
Tel: 02 9970 5111 Fax: 02 9970 5002
www.woodslane.com.au

This 2nd edition 2010
First edition published 2000 by Boiling Billy Publications
Text copyright © Vic Widman 2000 and 2010
Photographs © Vic Widman
Photographs © Craig Lewis/Boiling Billy Images
Photographs © Phil Richards & Liz Allwood pages 22, 67, 87, 153, 158, 161
Design & layout: Vanessa Wilton (Billy Boy Design)

This publication is copyright. All rights reserved. No part of this publication
may be reproduced, stored in a retrieval system, or transmitted by any
form or by any means electronic, mechanical, photocopying, recording or
otherwise, without the express written permission of the publisher.

If you have any suggestions for future editions of this book please write or
email us at:

Boiling Billy Publications
Locked Bag 1 Wyndham NSW 2550
Ph/Fax: 02/6494 2727
e-mail: info@boilingbilly.com.au
web: www.boilingbilly.com.au

National Library of Australia Cataloguing-in-Publication entry

Author: Widman, Vic
Title: Travelling the outback: the complete guide to planning and
             preparing your outback adventure / Vic Widman
Edition: 2nd Ed.
ISBN: 9781921606649 (pbk.)
Notes: Includes index.
Subjects: Four-wheel driving--Australia--Guidebooks.
             Four-wheel drive vehicles--Australia.

Dewey Number: 919.404
Printed and bound in China through Bookbuilders

All Boiling Billy and Woodslane Press books are available for bulk and
custom purposes. Volume copies of this and our other titles are available
at wholesale prices, and custom-jacketed and even mini-extracts are
possible. Contact our Publishing Manager for further information,
on **+61 (0)2 9970 5111 or info@woodslane.com.au**

contents

introduction vi

the outback travel dream............................. ix

ch 1   Planning Your Trip

getting started 1

when to start your planning 2

sources of information 4

access, permits & restrictions........ 6

time frames/rest days 7

travel distances............................... 10

your typical travel day 14

travelling with children................... 14

travelling with pets 18

holiday from hell or best ever
experience 19

ch 2   Preparing The Vehicle

selecting the right vehicle 23

    all-wheel verses four-wheel drive

    large or small four-wheel drive

diesel or petrol 25

auto or manual 26

tent or roof top tent or camper trailer
or caravan or motorhome 26

    tent

    roof top tent

    camper trailer

    caravan

    motorhome

making a good thing better 30

tyres 31

tyre pressure 32

one is not enough 33

tyre repair equipmemt 34

suspension 35

bull bars 38

rear bars 40

side steps or rock sliders................. 41

rear wheel carriers 43

fuel tanks 46

roof racks.. 50

roof rack storage bags/pods............. 53

storage systems/cargo barriers 53

power supplies.................................. 55

lights... 62

all the comforts of home.................. 63

spare parts.. 64

vehicle recovery equipment 64

**ch 3   Off-road Camper Trailers &
Off-road Caravans**

off-road camper trailers 69

off-road caravans 77

ch 4   Communication Equipment

what is it and do you need it?.......... 79

cb (citizen band) radio 79

uhf (ultra high frequency) radio 79

hf (high frequency) radio................. 81

satellite telephones.......................... 84

mobile phones................................... 85

personal locating beacon (plb) and
emergency position indicating radio
beacon (epirb) 85

global positioning system (gps)....... 85

spot.. 86

ch 5   Camping Gear

tents.. 89

roof top tents 91

swags... 94

air beds/mattresses 95

contents

sleeping bags 95
car fridges 96
camp lights.................................. 99
cooking stoves 99
cooking equipment 100
camp ovens 100
tables 101
camp chairs 101
portable showers and toilets........... 104

ch 6   Food & Water
quarantine restrictions 109
water 109
    containers.............................. 109
    quantities................................ 111
food 111
    plan a menu............................ 111
    meat 114
    fruit and vegetables................. 115
glass.. 115
cans 115
drinks 116
storage containers 116
some general hints on food storage and
meal preparation 118

ch 7   Personal Needs
clothing 125
washing clothes............................ 128
health 128
money 132

ch 8   Campsite Selection & Tips
how to choose a great campsite....... 135
camp fire tips.............................. 139

camping etiquette 142

ch 9   Outback Driving Tips
driving on unsealed roads.............. 145
unsealed roads and corners............ 146
controlling a slide.......................... 148
corrugations 148
passing oncoming traffic 152
overtaking in dusty conditions........ 153
wheel ruts 153
bull dust 154
tyre pressures 155
wet tracks in the outback............... 155
stranded in the outback 166

ch 10   Suggested Itineraries
where to go in one week 169
where to go in two weeks 170
where to go in four weeks.............. 172
where to go in six weeks 184
i'm retired – what about me?........... 190

ch 11   Your Outback Packing List 196

ch 12   References & Resources 208
index... 220
about the author 225

introduction

Ten years ago I wrote the first edition of Travelling the Outback. In the Introduction I spoke of the boom in four-wheel drive sales, the marketing of outdoor activities and how our financial status is contributing to this escapism that sees us travelling the outback.

Today little has changed. Despite the so called poor economic climate sales of four-wheel drives and related touring vehicles remain strong. In fact over the past 12 months the sales of caravans is said to have increased by 33% in some states. That is a huge leap!

No doubt, contributing to this situation is the fact that many so called baby boomers are now reaching retirement and finally, after a full and long working life, they are getting the chance to live their dream and tour the outback. You only have to take a drive up the Stuart Highway in winter to have this confirmed. The road is full of shiny new four-wheel drives and caravans with grey haired men and women at the wheel hopping from one caravan park to the next. The only problem with this is most caravan parks can't cope with the huge increase in outback wanderers and some find park life almost as claustrophobic as city life.

There has also been a big increase in the young families and couples making the big outback break, doing the lap or just taking 12 months off to go exploring before really settling down. These people are a little more adventurous than the usual grey nomad. The four-wheel drive is dressed to the nines with all the after market gear and they frequently venture down little used four-wheel drive tracks that crisscross our great country.

In some respects, despite this continued growth in outback travel from all quarters, the outback itself has remained static. It is still a wild and remote location, it still requires respect and plenty of pretrip planning and unfortunately people still perish on remote tracks and in some cases not all that far from civilised areas. The harshness that is synonymous with Australia is the one static item in this pool of adventure that we call outback travel.

The past ten years has seen enormous growth in safety devices such as global positioning systems, navigation systems and even remote communications. You can now have your entire route tracked and downloaded to Google maps viewable by your family back home for a just a couple of hundred dollars per year. There is really no need for anyone to ever wonder where you are, its all there at a click of the mouse. For example, I track my guides on their outback safaris for my four-wheel drive tour business using this equipment. In an instant I can tell if they are on schedule and exactly where they are located. Check it out at www.4wd.net.au

The internet itself has probably made the most advances since I typed the first edition of Travelling the Outback. If you can't find it on Google, well, it probably doesn't exist. Google won't help you too much when you're halfway across the Simpson

> **"** You can now have your entire route tracked and downloaded to Google maps viewable by your family back home for just a couple of hundred dollars per year... **"**

Desert but it does assist enormously in the all important pretrip preparation.

Despite what us seasoned travellers have seen in the way of improved information on outback travel and tremendous advances in car, four-wheel drive, trailer and caravan technology and capability, if you are new to outback travel it is still a jungle out there. The most common call I receive is "What 4WD should I purchase" closely followed by "I want to go around Australia, what should I include in my trip". Well, this new edition of Travelling the Outback will be your bible. But, even if you are a seasoned traveller, you will find snippets of information that will enhance your travels.

I've been travelling the outback for over 30 years now, leading four-wheel drive tours, writing about my adventures in various magazines and just exploring new country because its there. My knowledge on outback travel has continued to grow and develop throughout this time and no doubt will continue to do so for how ever long I can manage to Travel the Outback. I hope what I've learnt helps you to also realise your dreams and enjoy our fantastic country to its fullest.

Vic Widman

Sydney 2010

outback trips can be a family adventure

the outback travel dream

Fortunately most of us can still dream. We dream about winning lotto, we dream about not having to work to make a living and we dream about travelling the outback on our next holiday. Now, that holiday might be just a week or two of our annual leave or it may be a permanent holiday following our working life. Retirement does not mean nursing homes and dribbling in your beard, it can mean exploring the wonder of Australia's outback. Many younger people have a dream to go exploring before settling down. The outback is full of backpackers from Australia and overseas, living on a tight budget and yet seeing sights that few have ever seen before them.

Many travellers these days have their young children in tow. They have either taken leave without pay or simply quit their job and packed up the family to see Australia before life gets too serious. Renting out their home, buying a four-wheel drive and an off-road camper trailer, organising schooling for the kids whilst on the road, they have headed off for a year or two on their great dream.

Let me assure you, these dreams are well worth realising, if you have an urge to "find yourself" or to just escape the rat-race or if you have just retired, then go for it. The longer you wait, the more reasons you will find not to live your dream. Too many dreams have never been realised and sometimes if you don't grasp the moment then all can be lost. Our personal circumstances can change quickly and you can spend the rest of your life wondering "what if".

But a good dream that avoids becoming a nightmare is dependent on some planning and the gathering of worthwhile information. That is what Travelling the Outback is all about. It's taken me over 30 years to accumulate sufficient knowledge to say that I believe there is an art to having a great outback trip as opposed to a nightmarish trip. So hopefully this book will help you have the best time ever and realise your dreams.

blazing outback sunset

chapter 1

Enjoy the **Birdsville Track**

PLANNING YOUR TRIP

getting started

The success of any outback trip can be determined by the amount of planning that goes into it. In the very first instance you need to know exactly what you plan to achieve on your trip. Now, don't get me wrong, I have no problem with spontaneous decisions and in fact some of my best adventures have occurred as a result of a spontaneous decision to explore something that was not planned. But, in fact, it was planned, you see, building time into your itinerary to allow deviation from the planned route can be highly beneficial.

Let's start somewhere, and assume you have a great desire to see a certain part of Australia. However, there is little point in planning a drive through the Kimberley region if you live on the east coast and have only two weeks annual leave. So for most, there is always going to be time limits. In this case be realistic about what you can see in the time you have.

However, if you have taken 12 months off work or you have finally retired and just want to go on the wallaby (an Australian term for wandering around the countryside), then some planning will still help enormously. I've lost count of the number of times I've been asked to prepare a travel itinerary for someone who says they have three months and wish to do the Big Lap (the Big Lap is a round trip of Australia, something many grey nomads embark on each year). By the time I've written up their itinerary visiting all the iconic spots and the lesser known but usually more beautiful locations, the

itinerary is easily exceeding six months of travel and that does not include any rest days which must be taken. But, if you only have three months to do the Big Lap, yes, it can be done; it just means there will be places you simply won't have time to visit. So rather than be disappointed when you drive past that turn off up the coast, be prepared in your own mind, knowing that you are achieving your own goal and not those dictated by others.

So that is the point, take the time you have and set your self a goal that is achievable in this time. This book and its words of wisdom will help you determine exactly how to do that.

One of the greatest traps for those planning their trip is the detour problem. For example let's say you have decided to visit the Red Centre of Australia (an area usually bounded by Alice Springs and Uluru) during the winter school holidays. Assuming you live somewhere on the Australian coast, the first realisation is that just to reach Alice Springs you are faced with at least a four day drive. So four days out and four days back from a 14 day holiday is a pretty large percentage of time. But along the way you are passing some rather iconic spots such as the Flinders Ranges, so you decide to drop in there for a day or two. Then a mate mentions the Oodnadatta Track and the possibility of flying over Lake Eyre from William Creek. Well, of course you want to do that, there goes another four days. Suddenly, you've left yourself no actual time to see the Red Centre.

It is easy to take these detours when you are planning your trip, but, if you have any kind of time frame, then you need to discipline yourself to stick to your original goal. The more time you have to explore a particular area the more you will see, learn and remember. The grey nomad couple that take three months to do the Big Lap will have a great time but the couple who take 12 months will have an even better time. However, the couple that spends a week in the Red Centre will see more than the couple that spend a week driving from Adelaide to Darwin.

When determining how long you have for your dream holiday, don't underestimate the time it takes to get ready for your big trip. I don't mean the planning, I mean the actual packing and last minute arrangements for mail, watering the pot plants, arranging the pet minding and ensuring all the expected bills will be paid up. This little task

can take a few days. Just packing the vehicle, trailer or caravan can easily take a day or two. So allow time at the start of your trip. Equally, when you arrive home, give yourself time to unpack, clean all the camping gear and the vehicle, wash clothes and even sort through all those photo files before you head back to work. A few days at the end of a trip will take the stress away from the dreaded first day back at work!

So the lesson here is to allow time before and after your trip that is not included in the actual travel time, set realistic time frames for the type of travel you have in mind and choose a destination or theme for your trip and avoid the detours (but include a couple of days in case those detours actually add value to your original purpose for exploring the area you have chosen).

when to start your planning

Obviously you should start planning your trip as soon as possible. If you are planning a trip well in advance it will add to the knowledge you can gather. Knowledge is all important as it not only prepares you for what lies ahead but it also adds value to your trip.

If possible, start at least 12 months in advance. This is especially important from the point of view of determining the weather conditions that you are likely to encounter. A common mistake made by many people is the notion that a trip to our desert areas means hot dry conditions. In fact, most desert travel is undertaken in the winter months and it may come as a surprise to some that our desert regions frequently record temperatures below zero overnight. I have found that travel in the winter months in our desert regions in locations below the Tropic of Capricorn will usually see early morning temperatures in those idyllic desert campsites falling to below zero Celsius.

One memorable trip from Chambers Pillar to Alice Springs in July saw the temperature range during the whole day from zero degrees to just five degrees! However, in the following July I also experienced temperatures in the same region in the low thirties (Celsius).

Check the weather maps via the Bureau of Meteorology website www.bom.gov.au 12 months prior to your planned trip. This will give you a good idea of what to expect. Especially take note of any consistent wet weather patterns that correspond with your itinerary. Wet weather and unsealed roads in outback Australia usually mean no access. This can ruin your plans especially if only away for a short period.

By starting your planning as early as possible it gives you time to gather historical and current information on the areas through which you will travel. Don't just drive an outback road for the sake of saying "been there, done that". Drive it to learn about its heritage. There are numerous methods available to the modern traveller for gathering this information which is covered in the next subject matter.

Use your information planning to get the family or partner or friends who will be accompanying you involved in your trip. The more they know about the trip the more enthusiasm they will all show. Even if you are leaving loved ones at home, get them involved in your great adventure it adds to the enjoyment by all.

In this lead up time, especially 12 months prior when weather and road conditions will be most relevant, access the brains of those that have travelled before you. This is easily done via various forums and clubs. For example take a look at the forum section on www.exploroz.com.au it is a wealth of information.

Gather your history books that cover your route and read these well in advance, take notes of travel times, landmarks and conditions endured by our early explorers. On your actual trip you will see these come to life as you pass the same landmarks.

sources of information

If you are not computer savvy, then I'm afraid you are going to have to take some quick lessons on how a personal computer and the internet operates. In today's age of the internet and online information, you are simply missing out on too much not to be a little proficient in the use of the world wide web.

If you want to learn about a place just Google it. It doesn't matter what you are looking for these days, it can usually be found on the internet. Use

this service to your advantage. It will help you discover the history of an area, learn facts about it, find accommodation, establish what the fees are for certain areas, the list just goes on and on. For example, I recently noted from a Google map that there was a mine near Edith Falls in the Northern Territory. All I had was the name of the road leading to it, Mt Todd Road. So I Googled Mt Todd Mine and bingo I suddenly learnt all about the abandoned Mt Todd gold mine which was going to take $20m to clean up even though it had only been in existence since 1994.

The world of Google is probably the greatest advancement made for those of us travelling. This is closely followed by that unique website phenomenon known as the forum. Here, specialist websites provide an opportunity for those visiting the site to make comments. The best site for outback travel has to be the forum on www.exploroz.com.au Not only can you learn from people who have been there and done it

before you but there is an enormous amount of information on just about anything associated with Travelling the Outback.

This website also has many outback trek notes with helpful information on history, fuel availability, permit requirements and much, much more. As mentioned, you can Google explorers names and read from their journals, all found on the web, or better still, establish how to purchase their books and study them more closely.Don't forget the humble travel magazine either, most four-wheel drive, camper trailer and caravan style magazines include two or three travel stories each month. For example, I am writing a series of outback travel stories each month in Overlander Magazine and these can be used to help you gather the information you need to make your trip even better. The great Australian publications RM Williams Outback Magazine and the Australian Geographic Magazine also provide excellent material on the people who live and work in the areas through which you will be travelling.

I tend to keep an eye and an ear open on all the various sources of information including newspapers, magazines, radio and television. It is surprising how frequently a special place of interest might get mentioned. This information gathering adds to the excitement of the trip and the enjoyment when you finally get out there and see it for yourself.

In recent years there have been huge advancements in the quality and quantity of mapping information available. At the top of the tree in this respect is HEMA maps who are constantly driving around Australia and updating their mapping data. Of recent they have also produced some excellent books on particular areas that not only provide their maps but detailed historical and other relevant travel detail to the reader.

There are numerous other excellent Australian travel books also available, all of which contain up-to-date information and detailed maps usually with GPS coordinates to aid you finding significant locations.

Even the humble Tourist Information Centre or Visitor Centre will have a wealth of information that will prove useful. Visiting one of the numerous outdoor travel shows or caravan and camping shows that do the regular rounds of most capital cities and provincial centres is great value. Here you

Simpson Desert

will find most major tourist locations represented and you can easily collect their glossy brochures.

Remember, this planning can also take place whilst on the trip. Talk to people; ask questions, where have you been? What have you seen? Get to know the people in the Visitor Centres, they might just have that elusive snippet of information that makes a good trip great! I've even changed a tour itinerary based on a piece of information I learnt from a Visitor Centre whilst leading one of my recent four-wheel drive tours. The end result was discovering an amazing location on the coast near Ceduna that was voted as one of the highlights of the trip.

Fortunately, national park offices are becoming far more tourist orientated these days as well. Once again, most have websites where you can learn a lot of information but it's always best to talk to someone on the spot. Most rangers are only too willing to advise you on some great sights that the usual glossy brochures and websites make no mention. In addition, they will have firsthand, up to date advice on road and campsite conditions that could save you a lot of time.

access, permits and restrictions

Access to much of Australia is now controlled by one authority or another. This might be a simple case of applying online for a permit which costs nothing more than your time to fill in an application online, to others that require six months notification and come wrapped in numerous restrictions. When planning your outback travel it is a comforting feeling knowing that you have all of the necessary permits tucked away in the glove box and you won't live in fear of being asked to present your documentation by a ranger.

It may come as a surprise to some to learn that some areas of Australia are now off limits to travel by those of us seeking to fulfil our nomadic desires. Don't be tempted to flout the restricted access laws either as the fine print may include a hefty fine and confiscation of your vehicle.

What I have tried to do at page 212 is provide a comprehensive list of all the permits you will require for the various outback locations around Australia and how these might be obtained.

Unfortunately, any list like this with contact

ROAD CONDITION
DONOHUE H'WAY
IS CURRENTLY..
CLOSED
DRIVE SAFELY
DONOHUE HIGHWAY
DRIVE TO SUIT CONDITION OF ROAD
BULLDUST SECTIONS BETWEEN NORTHERN
TERRITORY BORDER AND BOULIA
OPEN TO 4WD WITH CARE
Please Drive Safely

numbers and email addresses is prone to change but it will serve as a good source of information to help you plan your next outback trip.

time frames/rest days

I've already talked about the crucial factor of time frames for your trip. As mentioned it is very easy to get carried away when planning your trip, there are just so many great places to visit in Australia.

So you have to be very disciplined, set your goal for your trip and don't be diverted from it if your time frame is tight. Of course if you have retired and have all the time in the world then by all means have a flexible plan and be ready to add to it as you go.

Another trap that many fall into is not realising just how big Australia is. Sure, you will always find someone who boasts how they drove from Melbourne to Cairns in three days, but did they see anything and how did they feel for the rest of their trip, exhausted I bet!

Having selected the region you wish to explore, and gathered as much information as possible it is now time to sit down and list all of your must see places. It is a good idea to prioritise these items once you have listed them as it may turn out that you simply don't have sufficient time to see and do everything. The lesson here is not to set a time frame that is too tight or, if your time frame is fixed, such as with annual leave, then don't have a priority list that is unachievable.

bird life converge to an outback river

Most importantly, remember that you are on holidays and are supposed to be relaxing and enjoying yourself. It is a good idea to build in rest days every so often. All that driving can become very tiring for the driver and tedious for the passengers, especially children. Allow at least one rest day from driving every seven days. Plan this rest day in a spot of interest such as a national park with walks, beside a billabong or even somewhere relaxing such as a seaside location. Apart from having a break from the driving you will really appreciate not having to break camp and pack up the tent/camper trailer. It also provides an opportunity for the children and yourself to learn more about the local area and explore the area in which you are travelling. The confines of a four-wheel drive restrict this 'hands on' approach to your travels. Spending a rest day in the outback often provides the opportunity for life long memories. For example, choose a billabong which will attract birds and wildlife, provide some shade and a ready supply of firewood.

When planning your trip you also need to allow time for mundane chores such as washing clothes, so don't plan them all in remote areas away from such niceties as running water and clothes lines, it's a sure-fire way to get offside with the other half if you make their life more difficult than it needs to be.

Any trip can be graced with vehicle maintenance issues or bad weather, so having a little spare time in your itinerary will allow for these eventualities which means they won't impact too severely on your achievement of your high priority goals. If

your outback travel entails a lot of kilometres don't forget that your vehicle will also need some down time to receive that all important servicing. On that point, don't expect to drop into an outback town and be able to get your vehicle serviced without notice. There are plenty of locals, farmers and other tourists who will be way ahead of you in the service queue. If you are booked into a major centre such as Alice Springs, Broome or Cairns, then also prebook your four-wheel drive for its grease and oil change before you leave home.

travel distances

Be realistic with the amount of distance you can travel each day. A run out to Broken Hill on the highway is vastly different to driving up the Oodnadatta Track from Marree. Highway cruising

MAYNE HOTEL

1888 – 1951

A popular resting-place for travellers, drovers, stockmen and opal miners to quench their thirst in the bar with drinks kept cool in the underground cellar nearby. The cellar was opened nightly to let in cool air and closed during the day to keep the hot air out.

Mayne Hotel ruins, outback Queensland

means good average cruise speeds and you can easily cover vast distances in one day. However, once you leave the sealed road your travelling times will vary greatly. As a rule and without any sightseeing you might be able to cover up to 600 kilometres on a sealed road in a day's drive (a day's drive is calculated on hitting the road around 8.30am and making camp around 4.30pm). However, on an unsealed road and again without any sightseeing this day's drive will usually only see you cover about two thirds of that distance or 400 kilometres. In desert country you might drive all day and be lucky to cover little more than 120 kilometres or far less if there are difficult tracks or soft sections. My shortest distance ever covered in one full day of driving from 8.30am to 4.30pm was just 12 kilometres in very difficult four-wheel drive terrain. So as you see, knowing a little about the area through which you will be travelling is going to assist you greatly.

However, most roads we travel also have some scenic or historic attractions along the way and if these have rated on your priority list of must see locations, then your travel distance per day is going to be severely affected. For example it is just 200 kilometres of unsealed road from Marree to William Creek, most people expect to cover this distance in around three hours. But along the way there are places to visit such as the Mound Springs, Coward Springs, Lake Eyre South and numerous Old Ghan rail sidings. The 200 kilometres will take the average motorist a full day of travel.

Your planning should identify the various scenic spots to be seen each day. Just think for a moment, how long does it take to stop the vehicle, walk to a scenic lookout, get your photos and return to the vehicle? If you are travelling with children, the simple act of unloading them and then strapping them back into the vehicle can be time consuming in itself. Also, the children don't just want to quickly walk to the lookout and then run back to the car, they want to play. All of this adds time to your travel day and unless you allow for it, you will be stressed by your own too tight time frame.

You also need to plan for the unexpected. Not everything you wish to see or expect will be listed in the travel brochures and you should allow time for what I call exploring. Take time to talk to the locals or other travellers to learn of those special places only known to them. If you see a side track, it may be worth exploring as these often lead to those idyllic campsites that make your trip more memorable.

Wet weather on our outback roads can strike at any time, even in the dry season it seems these days. Wet weather and unsealed outback roads are a bad mix. At worst you will find your progress slowed dramatically as a result of reduced speeds, assessment of flooded sections and deviations around those flooded areas. If the road you are travelling on has been closed to traffic due to wet weather, then you need to sit tight and wait for it to be re-opened or change your travel plans. Driving on closed roads is frowned upon by local shires and hefty fines now apply to anyone

ignoring a road closed sign and for good reason as your wheels will sink into the road surface leaving deep ruts which dry rock hard when the fine weather returns.

So how do you plan for these unexpected delays to your trip? Well, remember those rest days every week? Remember being realistic in setting appropriate travel times for the road ahead; remember planning to finish your day's travel well before dark? All of this planning will help you address the worst case scenario if it happens.

your typical travel day

Obviously this is going to vary depending on the location you're travelling through, your personal likes and dislikes for early morning starts, time in the driver's seat and even the weather. As a general rule try to be on the road by 8.30am, but remember that packing up the tent/trailer or caravan may take longer than expected, especially on the first couple of days.

Your travel day should allow for stops for morning tea and, of course, lunch. It's always nice if you plan to arrive at the new camp or destination by no later than 4pm allowing you time to set up camp in daylight and either relax around the camp fire before dinner or even explore the local area on foot before dark.

Catching sunrise in the outback can be a very special and even spiritual occasion so even though you may dislike early morning rises, if

you find yourself on a remote beach on Cape York, or camped beneath the red sand dunes of the Simpson Desert or overlooking a flooded Diamantina river in outback Queensland, you should try to experience the break of day firsthand.

travelling with children

The first bit of advice, is don't avoid your outback travel dreams because you have children, some of your best memories and theirs will derive from an outback trip with them.

There is a knack to travelling long hours in a vehicle with children. But, it does not always revolve around sticking a DVD player in front of them. Please don't do this, it may be used as a special treat or when there really is little to see, such as up the Stuart Highway from Port Augusta, but burying your children's faces into a mindless DVD is not teaching them anything. In fact, recent research has shown it may even be detrimental to their development.

Allow your children to have ownership of your trip, they are participating in it too so let them get something out of it. Include them in the planning so they know what is going on, even the real young ones can be involved in this planning stage, just bring it down to their level. For example, show them on a map where you are going, collect photos of animals and locations beforehand so they can identify these as they travel. For the slightly older ones get them to keep their own diary, write letters (yes, no emails) to their friends about their adventures. If you create a reason for them to look out the window, they will!

The usual games of 'I spy' and 'Something beginning with….' can help pass the time and keep their minds on what is going on outside. Pick up colour brochures in the towns you visit and let them have a look at them, they will get great enjoyment out of actually seeing the locations depicted in the brochure going past their window. Acquiring a stuffed toy (it might be a dog based on a cattle dog you have seen, or camel for the desert crossings, or even a sheep or kangaroo) either just before the trip or early in the trip provides a great playmate for them to experience the trip with. Get the little ones involved in the photography on the trip, use their new toy (or even a favourite toy from home) in the photos. Make a game of photographing the toy in all the great locations you visit. Not only is this something to keep their

minds interested on the trip, but also becomes a great keepsake when you return home. You can even create their own photo album and call it, for example, 'The Adventures of Carmella the Camel in Outback Australia'.

Having children on board means you need to build in plenty of stops to keep them active and interested. Try to stop at least every two hours and let the children have a run around, if passing through a town stop in a park where there may be swings or other play equipment, or at the very least plenty of open space to run around. Avoid the playgrounds in fast food outlets, as the attraction to purchase food will be too hard to avoid.

Take a ball or a frisbee or similar to throw around and play with the children. I led an outback trip once with a young family who had two children aged five and three years. Every time we

Bungle Bungle sunset

stopped dad would jump out and throw a ball and play with the children for 15-20 minutes. During this time mum prepared sandwiches and drinks in plastic bottles for them. When we jumped back into the four-wheel drives, the children were handed the food and drink, this kept them quiet whilst it was consumed and then they had a little sleep afterwards. Helped them through the long hours of travel and kept the children and the family happy.

School aged children also need entertaining but please leave the game boys at home, these mind numbing devices are not doing your children any good at all. Get them involved in collating information on the trip beforehand, have them prepare their own daily diary and then they can add to it as the trip progresses. Make your trip a learning and enjoyable one. Allow the children to read the history of a location to you as you travel rather than the other way around, let them be the teacher.

In the campsite let the children be involved with setting camp, if possible even allow them to carry their own tent and be responsible for setting it up. Whilst you don't want the children wandering off in the bush, you do need to encourage them to explore and learn about this new and foreign environment. The main thing is to set ground rules and where they can and can't go, and above all set rules on playing or running near any open fire you may have. Medical help out in the outback can be a long way away.

travelling with pets

If you have a pet dog, cat, bird or some other sort of pet, leaving it at home for long periods (or even just a short holiday) can be heart breaking for some owners. The pet is after all part of the family. However, travelling with pets is fraught with problems.

For starters national parks do not allow the entry of pet dogs or cats. There are obvious reasons for this; firstly the fear that the animal may escape their owners, become wild and hunt native wildlife; there is the hidden problem that the pet's scent will be left behind at campsites and places of interest which may deter native wildlife from visiting that area; and then there is the constant problem of their annoyance to other campers. In addition, poison baits are often laid in national and state parks to eradicate foxes and wild dogs, and it would be devastating if your family pet perished as a result of inadvertently consuming one of these baits.

Also, there is the added problem of caravan parks not being pet friendly, most don't allow you to bring your pet with you. Even in unmanaged campgrounds your pet may make itself unwelcome with other campers, and this can quickly develop into an ugly argument between the pet owner and the fellow camper.

For those who simply can't travel without their pet there are a few options, with some pet friendly caravan parks but this still does not address the issues of access to our most scenic locations found in national parks. Therefore, pet owners who wish to visit these scenic sites will have to find kennels or similar to leave their pets, which may require back tracking whilst on your trip. If this is an option for you don't forget to ensure that your pet's vaccination is up-to-date and that you carry the up-dated vaccination card.

Don't forget you will need to carry your pet's food, bedding and leads—and you also need to think of the pet's health on your trip. Keeping the pet couped up in the hot vehicle can be uncomfortable for the pet or even life threatening. Your pet will find the irritation caused by desert burrs and spinifex very distressing. The need to dispose of the pet's droppings correctly; checking your pet for possible ticks and other pests, all add to the problem of travelling with pets.

There are a couple of good websites devoted to travelling with pets, these might be able to help with planning your trip: www.holidayingwithdogs. com.au and www.doggyholiday.com

holiday from hell or best ever experience

It is all up to you really. If you put a little effort into the planning and start early, then you will have a great time. Ignore the advice above, have little idea of what lays ahead and forget to include the needs of those around you, then its likely that this may be your last ever outback journey. But, spend the time on researching where you are going, include the family in the planning, be realistic about your travel times and build in some flexibility and just like me, you could be going outback year after year. There is a magical attraction to the Australian outback, but you need to have time to see it and experience it. Whether you do this all depends on how you approach your trip. There is no excuse for getting it wrong—there is so much information available these days to help you—all it takes is a little commitment and understanding of what is needed.

Barramundi Gorge, Kakadu National Park

chapter 2

PREPARING THE VEHICLE

selecting the right vehicle

"What four-wheel drive should I purchase?" I am asked this question all the time. Is there one easy answer?

Well, yes, but whether that answer is appropriate to your particular needs may be questionable. One of the best four-wheel drives for touring outback Australia is the Toyota Landcruiser. But, is this the best vehicle for you? Well let's ask some questions first:

- Is this vehicle going to be your one and only vehicle?
- How many people will drive it and what type of vehicle do they usually drive (large or small, auto or manual, diesel or petrol)?
- How many people will you carry in it (at home and on holidays)?
- Where will most of its driving be done (to and from work in a capital city; purely on holidays; or a mix of city work and weekend escapes)?
- How often do you intend to go away in this vehicle?
- What type of four-wheel drive travel do you intend to do?
- How long do you intend on keeping this vehicle?
- How much money have you to spend?

So, if the Toyota Landcruiser is the best vehicle for outback travel what would make it unsuitable for you? Here are some simple answers, which will prompt more things for you to consider.

- If purchasing new or near new, you will need a considerable amount of money, anywhere from $60 000 to $100 000, just to purchase the vehicle. As you will see in this chapter, having another $10 000 to $15 000 spare cash to spend on this vehicle might also be required.
- The Landcruiser is a large four-wheel drive. If you live in a major city where parking and general travel is heavily congested this vehicle will become a chore. For example with a roof rack on, the Landcruiser won't fit into most multi-level car parks, or for that matter your own garage at home.
- If there are only two of you, why do you need an eight seater?
- If you only plan one annual holiday in the outback of say three weeks, and the rest of the

time you and your partner need an economical small car (each) to attend work and shopping, then how would you cope with one Landcruiser that struggles to fit into tight car parks?

- Have you any idea how much petrol a large four-wheel drive consumes in the city, or for that matter in low range, or crossing the Simpson Desert? Are you prepared to put up with the smell of diesel and greasy, smelly hands, every time you refuel your diesel powered Landcruiser?

On the other hand I could also pose these questions to you.

Q: What is the most reliable four-wheel drive on the market? **A:** *Landcruiser*.

Q: What four-wheel drive is the most capable in terms of outback travel? **A**: *Landcruiser*.

Q: What four-wheel drive is most commonly seen in outback Australia? **A:** *Landcruiser*.

Q: What four-wheel drive has the best resale value? **A:** *Landcruiser*.

I could go on but what I'm trying to portray is that there is no simple answer to the question *"What four-wheel drive should I purchase?"* It comes down to what your needs and expectations might be.

So, to help you with this vexing question let me discuss a few more pros and cons of outback travel.

If you are embarking on your one and only outback trip and never plan to do it again; this trip may include some of the iconic roads such as Birdsville Track, Oodnadatta Track and Gibb River Road. But you have no intention of crossing the 1000 sand dunes of the Simpson Desert or the 2000 kilometres of nothing but wasteland along the Canning Stock Route, then virtually any four-wheel drive, or for that matter, all-wheel drive should successfully complete your dream holiday and only with minor modifications (discussed shortly).

However, if you plan to travel the outback every year, cross all of our deserts and take the run up to Cape York, then you need a serious four-wheel drive with some extensive modifications to ensure a dream holiday every time.

To prove a point (and despite the fact that my own personal conveyance is a Toyota Landcruiser with virtually every conceivable modification which has crossed every desert in Australia), I recently assisted a mate purchase a second-hand four-wheel drive for just $10 000. To help the vehicle cope better with his dream holiday, we made some modifications to the vehicle costing in the vicinity of another $5000. Then given the age of the vehicle, we carried out some basic servicing which added another $2000 to the overall cost. So for less than $20 000 my mate had a great outback touring vehicle that took him and his wife on a fantastic three month trip around Australia towing their caravan. This was their once in a lifetime trip and it went off without a hitch.

all-wheel drive versus four-wheel drive

An all-wheel drive vehicle is one that does not have a low range transfer case. Its four-wheel drive selection may only be on demand (when the vehicle detects slippage at the normal drive wheels) with no option for the driver to select full time four-wheel drive). It generally is more car-like with lighter construction underneath the vehicle in terms of chassis, differentials and running gear. Also, the tyre size is more car-like than the larger four-wheel drive vehicles.

This means that the all-wheel drive is less capable off-road due to the lack of low range; its lighter construction means it can carry less weight and is more susceptible to damage from rough roads; and there is less availability of heavy duty tyres suited to off-road work. As a general rule an all-wheel drive

vehicle will not take you over deserts and across thousands of kilometres of corrugated roads.

A four-wheel drive will have low range capability, strong heavy under body components and drive train, large tyres and selectable full time four-wheel drive.

It is important to note that the availability of aftermarket equipment to enhance the vehicles' capability and your outback trip enjoyment is far more extensive for four-wheel drive vehicles than all-wheel drive vehicles.

large or small four-wheel drive

The decision here may be based on your use at home as much as it is based on your outback trip. However, the very reason that the small four-wheel drive is a great choice around town (nimble, easy to park, lightweight and economical) is what plays against it as a good outback tourer, where you want size and bulk to be able to stand up to the rigours of unsealed roads. Your outback tourer will also need plenty of space to carry your family and their camping equipment. If towing you need power and bulk to keep the camper trailer or caravan on track behind your four-wheel drive.

diesel or petrol

Gone are the days when a diesel motor was a real slug to drive (however, if choosing a second hand four-wheel drive anything over ten years old will fall into the slug category). These days diesel motors are equal to or greater in terms of power of their equivalent petrol varieties. Diesel vehicles return far greater economy and are far less prone to fuel use variation in tough four-wheel drive terrain. A diesel vehicle will provide greater engine compression braking in steep terrain than a petrol vehicle and a diesel motor has greater longevity than a petrol vehicle under constant use. Also, diesel is safer to carry and refuel from jerry cans than the volatile petrol.

The downside of a diesel vehicle is that its initial new price can be substantially higher than its petrol equivalent and refuelling a diesel can be a messy job due to the oily nature of the diesel that invariably adorns fuel pumps. The maintenance issue between petrol and diesel vehicles is no longer a big point of contention due to the relative cost of maintaining each type of motor over a prolonged period. However, what is becoming more evident is the need for clean fuel for the high pressure pumps used in diesel vehicles, any contamination of the diesel fuel can lead to expensive pump and engine rebuilds.

auto or manual

For outback travel use it makes very little difference if you drive an auto or manual. In fact, automatic transmissions provide a manual operation through the selection of ratios, so for outback roads and even sandy country either will perform well. In steep mountainous country an experienced four-wheel driver will generally prefer a manual diesel four-wheel drive as its low range engine braking is far greater than its equivalent automatic version. Fuel economy is slightly better in a manual vehicle

and if you choose a petrol version, this can make quite a difference in some driving conditions with the petrol auto being considerably less frugal.

It is interesting to note that some four-wheel drive vehicles no longer offer a manual transmission option. Even the mighty Landcruiser in its 200 series model only provides automatic. There seems little in the decision for auto or manual if you are going to spend a lot of time city driving in between your outback travels, then the automatic is going to be a far easier vehicle to live with and it is a better choice if towing heavy loads.

tent or roof top tent or camper trailer or caravan or motorhome

The next decision is to determine your means of accommodation. If you elect the four-wheel drive option only, then it means you will be taking a tent for those remote campsites. With a well equipped four-wheel drive and some training on how to use it, along with a tent or swag you can go virtually anywhere you wish, the only limit being government restricted access and your own self sufficiency ability.

tent

A good four-wheel drive and tent means you can truly explore the outback. Obviously the tent means you have to carry most of the comforts of home with you or adjust your standard of living slightly. Each day will require time to make and break camp, with everything you need to live

Outback travel accommodation options

tent

roof top tent

being packed away into the four-wheel drive. This reduces the space available in the four-wheel drive and the more people travelling with you, the more difficult this becomes. The tent can also mean that inclement weather can become a real challenge. This has to be weighed against the absolutely fantastic locations that you can reach that are only accessible by four-wheel drive. The tent is relatively cheap; with the total outlay for a tent, bedding and camp cooking gear rarely exceeding $3000.

roof top tent

A roof top tent is another means of achieving that go anywhere ability without the fear of sleeping with all the bities that frequent the remote locations that you prefer to camp in. Obviously your four-wheel drive has to be of sufficient size to

safely accommodate a roof top tent. Roof top tents range in price from $2500 to $4000 so it is a lot for just a bed under canvas. I will look at the tent/ swag/roof top tent options in more detail shortly.

camper trailer

A camper trailer hooked up to the rear of the four-wheel drive can overcome the hassles of a tent. Most are quick to erect, contain a few comforts of home that you might otherwise miss out on or compromise on with a tent, and provide a slightly higher level of protection from the elements. But be aware, there is a great variation in the range and quality of camper trailers. A camper trailer may merely be suited to sealed road towing, falling apart at the sight of a dusty corrugated road. Whereas others, designed for true off-road work, will relish the outback challenges. You will see

camper trailer

caravan

There are definitely boom times occurring in the caravan industry. Whilst most caravans are only designed for on-road use, there is an increasing number being marketed as off-road units. The caravan is virtually like towing a motel room behind you and they can boast all the comforts of home. If you intend to do a lot of travel and either just stick to the major tourist routes; or are prepared to carry a tent along with all the requisite camping gear so that on occasions when you head bush in your four-wheel drive you can leave the caravan in town, it may be the best of both worlds. For those that just can't leave the caravan behind no matter where they go, the off-road versions can certainly be towed down tracks such as the Gibb River Road, Birdsville and Oodnadatta Tracks, but once again they are not suited to the sand dunes

true off-road camper trailers in practically every corner of Australia. The downside of trailers is that their quality varies greatly and some can cause more problems than they are worth. A trailer can restrict where you venture, trailers are difficult to tow in sand dune country, in fact the Simpson Desert authorities ban tour operators from taking trailers, and would prefer that individuals not drag their trailers across the desert. Whist travelling in mountainous terrain an off-road trailer will severely impede your progress due to the extra load on the vehicle in steep terrain, and they can become very difficult to tow once the steep inclines and declines become wet with poor weather. A top quality off-road trailer can set you back $50 000+ so it is a big investment.

caravan off road variety

of the Canning or Simpson Desert. Prices for on-road caravans can range from $30 000 to $60 000+ whilst true off-road versions start from $50 000 and head north of $100 000 in some cases.

motorhome

Finally, the motorhome concept continues to grow in Australia. These vehicles are definitely on-road only, but some tow a small four-wheel drive behind them for running around town and day trips into nearby remote locations. These vehicles range from a room on wheels to a virtual house on wheels with prices to match starting from $120 000 up to in excess of $600 000 for the big plush units. These larger motorhomes are, in my opinion, fairly impractical in the Australian countryside being more suited to the giant American freeways and trailer parks. Simply finding somewhere to park one of these semitrailer type

motorhome

vehicles in the main street of our country towns can be a nightmare, and you really need to weigh up the huge financial outlay to get yourself into one of these units.

making a good thing better

Most four-wheel drives as they come straight off the showroom floor can be driven straight into the outback, but your trip and your comfort will be greatly enhanced if you spend a little time and money modifying the vehicle to suit the conditions you are going to traverse.

You may ask the question, why is it necessary to modify the vehicle that has just cost you anywhere from $30 000 to $130 000? The issue is that these vehicles, despite their go anywhere advertising rarely go off-road. To appeal to the greatest majority of purchasers vehicle manufacturers soften the vehicle for its on-road use, it is not considered necessary to design some components for the rigours of off-road use. Some equipment that is second nature to someone using the vehicle for outback use is not seen as necessary for a vehicle that will primarily be used in an urban environment.

It is estimated that less than 5% of all four-wheel drives sold in Australia are actually used in an off-road situation. If you were a vehicle manufacturer would you make the vehicle cost more by adding tyres suited to country that 95% of the owners will never drive on? Would you add expensive components and equipment that 95% of owners will never use? And would you provide a rugged and tough ride when 95% of owners are looking for a soft plush driving experience? So the vehicle is built for the majority of its owners rather than the 5% like, you and me, who want to explore our great country in a vehicle that has the capability to do so.

Let me take a look at the vehicle and tell you what you might consider attending to in order to make your escape machine just perfect for Travelling the Outback.

tyres

This is one of the key areas of a four-wheel drive and the difference between a great trip and a disaster. Make no mistake—the wrong tyre choice could kill you. Tyres not suited to the type of terrain through which you will travel could become damaged. This damage may become apparent immediately with a blowout, or it may be disguised as a slow leak which over time and use can lead to a catastrophic failure of the tyre possibly whilst travelling at freeway speeds – this may end in disaster.

The standard tyres supplied with your new four-wheel drive are designed primarily for highway use, remember those 95% of people who never go off-road? These tyres will provide a soft ride on-road, not create a lot of road noise and are designed to have reasonable grip on the highway. This on-road design may compromise their ability to withstand the rigours of outback travel. They may be soft in the sidewalls which could lead to

damage in this key area and their close tread pattern will not work as efficiently on loose gravel, rock and in particular in mud.

You need to be aware that your tyres are the contact point between you and the road surface and as such the tyres will be subjected to the harshest treatment. Unless you put some thought into your tyre choice you are likely to spend a lot more time repairing tyres than enjoying the scenery.

So, whilst I don't recommend using your highway terrain tyres in the outback, I also don't see any need to waste them, keep them for when you come back home and the vehicle is reassigned to its daily duties. But I do suggest you have either an all terrain or mud terrain style tyre available for your outback adventure. This style of tyre generally has a stronger construction, especially in the sidewall, will also have a more rugged and open tread pattern which will aid grip in loose gravel, rock and especially mud, and they actually wear longer than a standard highway design tyre.

As I have travelled virtually every four-wheel drive road and track in Australia over my 30 years of outback exploring, you can imagine that I've seen some good and not so good tyres in my time. It's fairly easy these days to work out what is the best choice for your particular vehicle and terrain you intend to travel through. Just go onto any of the many forum sites in clubs, magazines or speciality travel websites and ask the question. Talk to the experts who do a lot of outback travel, take note of what they are using. For example, in my four-wheel drive tour business, do you think I want to be constantly let down by poor tyre choice?

tyre pressure

If there is one key issue I have learnt over my years of outback travel, it is that you need to be very aware of your tyre pressures and be prepared to adjust them to suit the conditions. I now have a tyre pressure monitoring system installed in my four-wheel drive and can monitor the pressure of each individual tyre as I drive. This one feature could save my life; as a slow leaking tyre whilst driving up the Oodnadatta Track will soon drastically overheat – leading to sudden failure of the sidewall. A blowout of this type, at speed, on a loose surfaced road is the single biggest cause of motor vehicle accident due to component failure in the outback. Remember, a roll over at 70kph in the outback can at worse be deadly, and at least will ruin your holiday and your vehicle.

So what tyre pressure is right for you? That is an impossible question. But what I can advise is, that the old cliché of 'when you load the vehicle pump up the tyres', does not go with off highway driving. As a general rule I suggest that no matter how

heavily loaded you may have your four-wheel drive, you should drop your tyre pressure to below 40psi once you leave the sealed road. This sole action will reduce your likelihood of sustaining a flat tyre by more than ten fold.

Independent tests have shown that the lower the tyre's pressure the more flexible and compliant the tyre is over objects that may otherwise pierce through the rubber. Of course, on good gravel roads like the Birdsville Track, you don't need to have tyre pressures any lower than say 25psi as the rotating tyre at speed will generate enormous heat in a tyre whose sidewall is flexing. Remember that blowout I wrote of on the Oodnadatta Track, that was a result of the tyre deflating and flexing so much that it overheated and the sidewall literally melted.

I have found for my vehicle that tyre pressures between 30 and 35psi on good gravel roads works well. Where the terrain becomes rockier and slows progress, it is suggested that you drop tyre pressure even further

adjust tyre pressures for off highway driving

with many off-road experts finding 25psi as an ideal pressure in this type of terrain. Of course if you are in sandy terrain forward progress will most likely cease if you have more than 20psi in your tyres. The tyre needs to float over the soft sand rather than sink into it. Generally for sand driving maintaining your tyre pressure between 15 and 20psi will be sufficient to maintain easy forward progress.

Another essential for off-road use is a good tyre pump so you can inflate your tyres to the desired pressure when you leave the unsealed roads behind. Don't drive on partially inflated tyres at speed on sealed roads. Use a good tyre pump to return them to the manufacturer's recommended pressures when you hit the black top.

one is not enough

If you intend to travel into remote locations such as the Simpson Desert, Canning Stock Route or even Cape York, it is highly recommended that you carry two spare tyres for your four-wheel driver. This is a safety issue, as getting stuck in a place like Durba Springs on the Canning Stock Route with two ruined tyres can become a very expensive exercise, if not possibly life threatening. Don't fall into the trap of carrying an extra spare that is near the end of its life either. It is important that all tyres are in the best possible condition for the road ahead. Remember, the spare on the roof can suddenly become the main contact point between you and the road with no backup.

If you are towing a trailer, and its tyres are the same size as the tow vehicle, then your spare for the trailer and the spare for the four-wheel drive will suffice.

The second spare should be mounted on a rim, ready to be used. However, this combination is very heavy and presents its own problems in respect of where to carry it on the four-wheel drive and actually handling it to this location. For example if stored on the roof rack, the second spare may require two people to actually lift it up or down.

Alternatively, if you have the appropriate equipment and know how to use it, you may only need to carry the extra spare tyre and not the rim. This reduces the weight of the extra spare considerably. It does mean that you will need to have a tyre repair kit including tyre levers and equipment to remove he tyre from the rim and

carrying two spare tyres

reseat the tyre once repaired—if and when it is required—plus an air compressor with suitable pressure output to re-seat the bead of the tyre. The equipment available for this purpose these days makes this a relatively easy task although if you intend to be self-sufficient in this respect I strongly recommend you practise using the equipment before departing on your outback journey. Be aware that some 18 inch or larger tyres are very difficult to change in the bush using this gear and this may prove to be impossible.

If your vehicle is equipped with split rims your tyres will have tubes fitted inside the tyre carcass. Any flat or slow leak will require removal of the split rim and the tyre from the rim to patch the tube. This makes the task of tyre changing and tyre repair far more difficult than tubeless tyres. In fact, changing tyres on split rims can be a dangerous exercise, especially the re-seating of the bead. There have been some awful accidents with split rims flying off the rim under pressure as the tyre is inflated. I suggest leaving this task to the experts in a tyre repair workshop.

Whilst talking of tube tyres, the most common incident of a flat tyre with a tube tyre is the result of inspection stickers being left on the inside of the new tyre carcass. This small sticker rubs against the tube as the tyre rotates, either wearing a hole in the tube or melting at the contact point with the heat generated by the rubbing. If you are getting new tyres fitted to your split rims, I suggest you actually inspect the inside of the tyre before they are mounted on the rim to ensure these small

stickers are removed. I have found that you can't trust the tyre supplier to attend to this detail.

Finally, in relation to tube tyres, your spares kit should consist of various sized tube patches, tyre scrapers and necessary glue to attach the patches. Carrying a spare tube is not a bad idea either but be aware, that spare tube you have had stored in the garage for this purpose for the past few years has probably deteriorated with age. Tubes should be renewed every 24 months at most if not used.

tyre repair equipment

I have already mentioned the availability of tyre repair kits, these consist of a set of jaws used to break the bead of the tyre off the rim. They also include tyre levers, although it is a good idea to have at least three tyre levers in your kit. I suggest you add a rubber mallet to the kit to allow for some help without damaging the rim or levers. You will also need replacement valves and a valve remover.

Tubeless tyres are far easier to repair if you have a simple nail or sharp stone that has penetrated the tread area of the tyre. This can be repaired without the need to dismount the tyre from the rim. Using a tyre plug kit the operation can be completed in a matter of minutes. The tyre plug kit will consist of a reaming tool, a split pin style tool, a number of sticky rubberised tyre plugs and some vulcanising glue. The sticky plugs are threaded through the split pin tool which is pressed into the hole (after reaming it) and as the split pin tool is withdrawn the sticky plug, which you have previously smeared

tyre plug

with glue remains in place. The tyre can then be reinflated and ready for use. Be aware that this is an emergency repair only and all tyres repaired in this way should be inspected by a qualified tyre repairer as soon as possible.

There is no point equipping yourself with all the appropriate tyre repair equipment and then not carrying a suitable air compressor. A suitable air compressor is one that will have the ability to pump enough volume of air to re-seat the bead of the tyre on the rim. Many smaller volume pumps are fine for inflating and deflating tyres for off-road and sand use, but fail to have the ability to re-seat the bead on a tyre. So if you are investing in a tyre pump, spend a few more dollars and acquire a pump that will do this, and then practise with it before leaving home.

suspension

Working our way up the vehicle, the next area to consider is the suspension. As previously mentioned, your showroom floor four-wheel drive has been built to handle the occasional speed hump in a suburban back street more so than

a thousand corrugations up the Old Telegraph Road on Cape York. As a result the springs tend to sag when the vehicle is fully loaded with all your camping gear, food, water and fuel for your outback trip. The standard issue shock absorbers are quite thin and have minimal oil capacity and valving, therefore they tend to overheat very quickly with extended use on corrugations. Once the shock absorber has over heated, the oil within the shock tends to boil and aerate, drastically reducing the ability of the shock absorber to absorb the bouncing effect of the springs on the vehicle. When this happens the four-wheel drive becomes very soft on its suspension, and tends to bounce and wallow, to a point where it either becomes uncontrollable or the ride is similar to being in a small boat on a choppy sea, passengers

heavy duty suspension upgrade

outback roads can be tough on suspension components

have known to become car sick (similar to sea sickness) because of the soft ride.

Older four-wheel drives, those that have travelled more than 50 000 kilometres on standard shock absorbers and springs, quickly demonstrate this trait when they hit an unsealed road. At this stage the shocks are already partially beyond their serviceable life. This is a recipe for disaster on any outback trip involving unsealed roads.

There are few vehicles on the market that will not respond positively to upgrading their suspension. I have lost count of the number of people that have followed my advice in respect of upgrading their vehicle's suspension and remarked on the improved ride and road manners of their four-wheel drive, even on the highway.

So, what is involved with upgrading your vehicle's suspension? Firstly you need to consult an expert in the field. Most of the major four-wheel drive accessory outlets and workshops will be able to assist in this respect. The sales person should be asking you what style of driving you will be doing, the typical load you will be carrying and what accessories you have or are likely to fit to the vehicle. For example if you plan to fit a steel bull bar, electric winch, driving lights and a couple of UHF radio aerials to the front of the vehicle, all this weight will affect the front springs and the replacement spring needs to take this into account.

The springs on the vehicle may consist of a coil spring, or a torsion bar style spring – what is

known as a leaf spring – or a combination of these different spring types. An upgrade to the spring usually means total replacement of the original item with a spring that is stronger, thicker and more tightly wound (in the case of coil and torsion bar springs). Its purpose is to slightly raise the vehicle (it is suggested that this not exceed 50mm) and be capable of supporting the weight of the vehicle when fully loaded without excessive sagging. (Local vehicle registration authorities may dictate the ride height adjustments that are permitted). This will give the vehicle slightly improved ground clearance on its body components which in turn improves what is known as the entry and exit angle of the vehicle in more rugged terrain (entry angle is where the front of the vehicle comes into contact with the ground and exit angle is where the rear of the vehicle, usually the rear bumper, scrapes on the ground).

The shock absorber is designed to stop the spring from bouncing after it absorbs the impact of the wheel hitting a pot hole, rut or other undulation in the road surface. Without the shock absorber or one that is working efficiently the vehicle will continue to bounce, making it uncontrollable. The replacement shock absorber needs to have sufficient length to compensate for the slightly longer travel created by the raised suspension and, equally important; it needs to have a greater capacity to work longer under harsh conditions without fading and ceasing to do its cushioning effect. The shock absorber takes the bounce out of the spring, the quicker it can do this, the more control the driver will have.

Aftermarket shock absorbers designed for heavily loaded four-wheel drives usually have a greater capacity in the internal chambers of the shock absorber, therefore they have more fluid (in this case oil). Obviously with more oil to dissipate the heat generated by the spring bouncing the aftermarket shock absorber will continue to do its work for a longer period and is able to cool down quicker than a standard small bore shock absorber. This larger size also allows for more valving inside the shock absorber through which the oil passes, thus aiding its cooling effect and dampening of the bounce effect created by the spring.

A vehicle fitted with aftermarket springs and shock absorbers can endure our Australian outback roads with ease, but this is not to say they will not fail and sometimes this can be in very dramatic circumstances. I have seen excellent aftermarket shocks literally explode into pieces due to the severity of the corrugations. The Canning Stock Route is one track that can be very harsh on a vehicle's suspension. For this reason, I recommend that you also carry at least one front and one rear replacement aftermarket shock absorber in your spare parts bin. I would also suggest you keep in your spare parts bin some replacement rubber or polyurethane washers for the shock absorbers and leaf springs (if fitted) as these can be easily replaced on the track if they fatigue or fail.

Another alternative method to compensating for sagging suspension, especially when hooking up a trailer or caravan is the fitting of air bags to the rear springs. This is not a replacement for aftermarket springs and shocks and will not improve the longevity of your shock absorber on corrugated roads. The air bag comprises two strong polyurethane bags connected to an air hose which allows you to pump up or deflate the air bag as required, thus raising or lowering the rear of the vehicle by a few millimetres. The hose line and air bag may be vulnerable to chafing or staking and once a leak commences the full effect of the air bag may be lost.

Please be aware that some vehicles with air suspension cannot have their suspension modified in this way, in this case you need to rely on the existing suspension to do all the work, not always an ideal situation. Also, you should check with your local motoring authority in relation to the legalities of altering the suspension on your vehicle as there are stringent parameters which you must stay within.

bull bars

The main purpose for fitting a bull bar to your vehicle is to protect it against an animal strike. Once you leave the confines of the city and start to travel our magnificent countryside the chances of colliding with an animal increase dramatically. Kangaroos are the main culprits although on some outback roads emus, and even wild goats can be a constant menace. In unfenced farmland wandering stock including sheep (who are particularly dumb when it comes to crossing the road) and cattle are a major issue. Hitting a fully grown Brahman bull at any speed is going to cause major damage to your vehicle if it is not protected by a bull bar.

There are generally two choices when it comes to bull bars. The steel bar or the alloy bar. Some plastic style bull bars are also available however, whilst they have the ability to deform and then reshape into a near original condition, it is the initial deformation that may cause serious damage to your vehicle.

A steel bull bar will provide the best protection in most cases as it tends to push the animal away from the vehicle, and is strong enough not to suffer massive deformation which may result in panel or worse, radiator damage. The downside to a steel bull bar is its weight and the

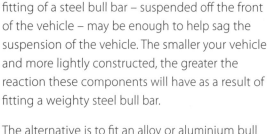

fitting of a steel bull bar – suspended off the front of the vehicle – may be enough to help sag the suspension of the vehicle. The smaller your vehicle and more lightly constructed, the greater the reaction these components will have as a result of fitting a weighty steel bull bar.

The alternative is to fit an alloy or aluminium bull bar. These are naturally much lighter than the steel unit and will have less affect on the suspension components. However, in a severe impact with an animal, the alloy is more prone to cracking with deformation and whilst it may do the job of protecting the vehicle from serious damage it may also mean that an insurance claim will still require submission to replace the now damaged bull bar.

A quick word on how to avoid an impact with an animal. For kangaroos, the old rule of avoiding driving at sunrise and sunset still applies as this is the time that kangaroos and wallabies are most active. Night travel on quiet country roads also seems to attract more than its fair share of kangaroos and if possible avoid travel at this time. Unfortunately a kangaroo strike can occur at almost any time of the day and I have said for a long time that the kangaroo you hit is the one you don't see until the last minute. This is because they have a tendency to be off the road amongst the bushes, when scared by the noise of your vehicle they scamper in all directions and can suddenly appear from between bushes and try to dart across the road. I've even had a kangaroo jump into the side of my vehicle, not seeing it at all until it scrambled off the road after scaring the daylights out of me with a sudden and loud thud on the side of my Landcruiser.

If you see a kangaroo standing on the road you should apply the brake evenly and continue to steer straight ahead. Too many accidents have occurred as a result of people taking evasive action and losing control of their vehicle, regretfully some people have even died as a result of an accident whilst avoiding a kangaroo. Brake steadily and steer straight ahead remaining on the road, this is particularly important if you are towing a camper trailer or caravan. The kangaroo is very likely to jump clear at the last moment anyway and if you take evasive action there is a 50/50 chance that you will still hit it.

Emus are nearly as dumb as sheep, in fact they are possibly more stupid. If you see an emu off the road slow down, because you can almost guarantee that even though it may be up to 100 metres away, it will run directly in front of your vehicle at some time. It is better to slow right down and watch the emu run than to risk damage to your vehicle.

Sheep need to be treated with great care too, if you see sheep grazing beside an unfenced road, you can almost guarantee that they will decide to cross the road in front of you. Because sheep follow sheep, there can sometimes be a constant stream of sheep running from the safety of one side of the road across your path to the other side of the road. Slow down when you see sheep and again

be prepared for the last half dozen to dash across, literally, metres in front of you.

Cattle are slower moving, but you don't want to hit a big bovine, that will almost certainly bring your holiday to an end. Cattle are far more stubborn too, and tend to stand on the road and try to stare you down, so be prepared to come to a full stop if you see cattle on the road or close by. Young calves require particular attention as they tend to be spooked by the vehicle and often run directly across your path.

If you do hit an animal it is very likely that it will scamper off into the bush or night, it is unlikely that you will find it, even though it may be severely injured. However, if the animal is disabled on the road or beside it, it is more humane to guard it from other vehicles, birds of prey, foxes and dingos than to leave it to be scavenged. If near a local town, then send for help by the local Police or wildlife organisation. If no help is available it is more humane to put down an injured animal than to leave it to the elements and scavengers. However, be aware that an injured animal can be very dangerous and you should always consider your own safety when attending to this type of situation.

rear bars

Continuing in the vehicle protection mode, some vehicles have the opportunity to replace their rear bumper bar with something a little more solid. On my Landcruiser I have taken off the flimsy plastic rear bumpers, which really won't protect the vehicle from any major impact, and replaced it with a steel Kaymar Engineering rear bar. Whilst this adds considerable weight to the vehicle I have to admit that it has been used on a couple of occasions and I'm glad it is made of a solid material.

The primary use is protection of the rear of the vehicle and in some rugged four-wheel drive applications such as dropping into a cut away creek crossing or a severely eroded track it is not uncommon for the rear bumper to catch the ground. The standard issue plastic style bumper will easily fold up, and apart from looking untidy from then on they are expensive to replace with the standard issue bumper.

My steel bumper has withstood the weight of the vehicle coming down on it and I could even use it as a jacking point to lift the

heavy duty rear bumper

weight of the vehicle in the event of being bogged or trapped in a rut. Good replacement steel rear bars have solid, safe vehicle recovery points and vehicle jacking locations. In the event of someone running into the rear of your vehicle or you accidentally reversing into a tree or embankment, I can assure you that your vehicle will suffer far less cosmetic damage with the steel rear bumper than the standard issue plastic bumpers.

As mentioned the downside is the extra weight that the rear bumper will add to your vehicle, but if you have had your suspension correctly set-up then this is not an issue. Only purchase replacement rear bars from well known and reputable four-wheel drive companies and ensure that they are correctly fitted to your vehicle using the appropriate high tensile rated bolts, especially if you use the recovery points located on the rear bar.

side steps or rock sliders

Further on the vehicle protection theme, the next item to consider is the humble side step. Most four-wheel drives will have some form of side step fitted as standard. These are usually made of aluminium or tough polyurethane like material. Neither of which will withstand an impact with the ground on a rough four-wheel drive track. They often become banana shaped and are quite unsightly for the remainder of their life. The actual worth of these standard side steps as an aid to enter and exit the vehicle might also be questioned. They tend to be quite narrow and partially hidden under the sill or

side rails

of actually dislodging the whole wheel arch, not a good look. The aftermarket industry has attempted to provide a better solution, and whilst not available for all vehicle makes, it's worth checking what is available for your specific four-wheel drive.

Replacement side steps or rock sliders as they have become more commonly known are designed to be strong and tough without reducing the ground clearance of the vehicle. Predominantly made of steel, they can withstand a hefty impact without deforming or dislodging. Generally they also provide a greater foot platform, thus actually aiding entry to and exit from your vehicle. Some of these side steps have rails that extend up and over the front wheel arch as seen on my own Landcruiser. These side rails provide protection for the front guard and on a slippery, muddy trail it is not uncommon for the vehicle to slide into the roadside embankment, my side rails have saved my front guards from damage on these occasions. Once again, the downside is the extra weight, and on some occasions I've actually had sticks flicked up by the front wheel and become lodged between the side rail and the front guard causing some minor cosmetic damage to the front guard.

body work of the vehicle and hence this restricts the area available for your foot when entering the vehicle.

Another downside of the standard issue side step is they actually tend to reduce the ground clearance on what is known as the ramp over angle of the vehicle. Hence the underside of the side step is the first point of contact with the ground, and due to their light construction, they either bend or tear out the mounting brackets leaving the side step unattached at one point. Of more concern for off-road use is the side step that is moulded into the wheel arches. If you happen to catch one of these side steps on the ground you stand a good chance

If the majority of your four-wheel driving is done in mountainous terrain where tracks are very rocky, or can become wet and muddy, a set of side rails combined with rock sliders (side steps) would be a good investment. It's also fair to say that the steel side rail would provide additional protection from an animal strike.

rear wheel carriers

Many four-wheel drives carry their spare wheel under slung at the rear of the vehicle. The Landcruiser is a prime example. For off-road use or outback touring this is an impractical location. Often the spare wheel is the lowest point of the vehicle, and on steep exit angles, in soft sand or in mud it is the first item to contact the ground. I have seen spare wheels actually torn from their mounting brackets under vehicles and left on the road as the driver drove on blissfully unaware that they had just ripped out their spare wheel.

Using the sidewall of your spare wheel as a grader on the track is not real sensible either as it may actually damage the tyre rendering it useless when most needed.

In addition, becoming bogged in muddy terrain and then suffering a flat tyre as well (I've seen it happen several times) means that you may be unable to actually retrieve the spare wheel without considerable jacking of the vehicle in the first place, plus its covered in wet oozy mud, not a pleasant job at all.

I have also found that spare wheels mounted on the rear door may, over time, cause fatigue to the hinges of the door. This is due to the extra weight of the spare wheel and the combined effect of vibrations caused by driving on corrugated roads. Once the door starts to drop or stretch its hinge bolts, the dust sealing is severely impacted and in a worse case scenario, the rear door hinge may actually fail.

In these circumstances, mounting the spare wheel on a wheel carrier at the rear of the vehicle will make a lot of sense. This gets it out from under the vehicle thus overcoming; the grounding issues, its removal in difficult circumstances, and the general poor state of the spare tyre when on a greasy muddy trail. It also alleviates the possibility of damage to the rear door hinges where it is mounted directly to the door.

The spare wheel carrier is either attached to the chassis of the vehicle with a bar that goes over your existing plastic rear bumper, or, if you have taken my advice on replacement rear bumpers, it will be integrated into the rear bar. This combination replacement rear bar and spare wheel carrier is far from a cheap alternative, but if you

spare wheel carrier

Gosse Bluff, Central Australia

intend to do a lot of off-road travel you will soon realise the huge benefits they offer.

There is another great advantage to having your spare wheel mounted on a wheel carrier, checking the tyre pressure in your spare suddenly becomes a very easy task.

The downside, apart from the high cost, is that you now have a rear wheel carrier that needs to be unlatched and swung away every time you need to access the rear of the vehicle. Also, some aftermarket wheel carriers do not withstand the rigours of off-road use, especially corrugations, and may fail. Fortunately not all wheel carriers are the same, for example I have never had any issues with the Kaymar Engineering wheel carrier on my Landcruiser.

fuel tanks

Most of Australia's major outback tracks have great distances between fuel stops. With your four-wheel drive fully loaded for an outback trip your fuel economy is not going to be at its best. If your chosen track involves sand driving such as across the Simpson Desert or up the Canning Stock Route, then your fuel consumption is going to suffer. Although diesel vehicles exhibit only minor variation in fuel usage depending on the terrain, petrol variants can have huge differences in fuel consumption. A day spent on say Stockton Beach near Newcastle in New South Wales, can return horror fuel consumption figures in some big petrol engine four-wheel drives. I've seen figures of 60

litres per 100 kilometres recorded at times on some petrol vehicles. Even in the Victorian High Country where there is no sand but a lot of low range work, petrol vehicles can really guzzle the fuel.

There is a trend these days to reduce the size of standard fuel tanks in modern vehicles, possibly to give more floor space for occupants. You have to remember these vehicles are not actually built with travelling Australian outback roads as their primary application.

The end result is you will need to carry extra fuel at some stage. Without doubt the best method of carrying additional fuel is to have your vehicle fitted with a long range fuel tank. From the point of view of ease of use, safety and convenience a long range fuel tank is a far better option than carrying your extra fuel in jerry cans. However, the very high cost of these long range tanks requires careful consideration. If you only need 40 or 50 litres of extra fuel, the cost of two jerry cans is far less than a long range fuel tank. If this trip is going to be your one and only outback sojourn, then the viability of outlaying a large swag of money as opposed to less than $100 really needs careful consideration.

If you are setting up your vehicle for numerous outback journeys then the question of the economics of investing in a long range fuel tank becomes a little easier to answer. I guess this is the ultimate answer—if you are going to get value out of the investment in a long range fuel tank, then this is the best choice. If however, you only need to carry extra fuel on one or two occasions then the option of a few jerry cans becomes more attractive.

If going down the long range fuel tank option, there are not a lot of pitfalls. Although, the old adage of sticking with well known brands still applies. The best option is the replacement of existing fuel tanks with a larger variety; this makes use of existing fillers, gauges and fuel lines. The less disturbance of the standard equipment the better. Some vehicles do not allow space for the standard tank to be replaced in which case additional fuel tanks are installed. Here, you need to have a thorough understanding of how the fuel is transferred from one tank to the other or whether the vehicle draws its fuel direct from the new tank. This is important so you know where to start looking if there is a fuel problem whilst out on the track. Once again, the less new components the better the system will be, this is based on the theory of there is less to go wrong or become faulty. Another point to be aware of is the ability of your vehicle to draw on all the fuel that is in the fuel tank (standard or long range). Some vehicles may hold 140 litres of fuel but only

125 litres is useable. It is wise to run your tank down until the vehicle is having difficulty drawing more fuel and then refilling it to gauge exactly how much fuel is useable.

If you decide to carry any extra fuel in jerry cans then a few precautions need to be taken. Firstly the choice of fuel container is very important. The number one rule is only use containers that are marked as fuel safe. Use of other styles of container can lead to leaking and possible fire through static ignition. If you need to carry diesel fuel it is far less volatile than petrol. However, it will still burn given sufficient heat and flame. Spillage of diesel, whilst not as likely to create a fire, does leave you with an oily, smelly mess and this needs to be considered if you elect to carry fuel inside the vehicle or on the roof rack.

Petrol on the other hand is extremely volatile and caution needs to be exercised when handling petrol jerry cans and refuelling with them. You don't get too many second chances with a petrol fire. Petrol fuel vapours also need to be treated with the utmost caution. Petrol vapours from refuelling with a jerry can have been known to cause numerous fires. Always avoid refuelling near any naked flame, this includes cigarettes, camp fires, gas stoves and even the pilot gas light in some three way car fridges. On my four-wheel drive tag-along tours I have a rule that anyone refuelling with petrol from a jerry can needs to be 100 metres away from the campsite or any other vehicle/camper, down wind of the camp and have a fire extinguisher at the ready.

I have even seen a petrol vapour explosion occur where jerry cans were being filled up at a local service station in a confined space. As the fuel nozzle was removed from the steel jerry can, the lip of the can was touched by the steel nozzle, causing a spark which ignited the fuel vapours. For this reason I prefer to use the tough polyurethane style fuel containers rather than the steel type jerry can.

The big mistake a lot of people make when carrying their extra fuel in jerry cans is to carry it well before it is needed. This only adds extra weight to the vehicle and the increased potential for leaks or damage to the fuel container or the roof rack where it is being carried. My suggestion is that you only fill your jerry cans just prior to when they will be needed. For example, if you are doing a Simpson Desert crossing from west to east, then either fill your fuel containers at Oodnadatta or Mt Dare, there is no need to carry

all that extra fuel and weight from home. The few dollars saved by purchasing cheaper fuel at home will soon be cancelled by the extra weight on the vehicle leading to higher fuel consumption, and if the rigours of outback travel take their toll on the vehicle or the roof rack due to this extra weight, then that cost will easily out weigh any saving with the use of cheap fuel.

The storage of jerry cans present another obstacle. The most common location is on the roof rack. However, whilst this is by far the most preferred location you need to consider the weight of the fuel and how your roof rack will cope with it. For example, if you just have one or two 20 litre jerry cans, the weight, whilst hefty, should cause no problem to your roof rack. However, if you are carrying more than a couple of jerry cans, then their weight when full will be considerable and may easily exceed the roof rack's load capacity. Most vehicle manufacturers will have a recommended load capacity for the rails to which the roof rack might attach, and in some cases this is quite low. If you exceed the load capacity of either the roof rails or the roof rack, then failure of these items is very likely, especially when the load is being carried on unsealed corrugated roads or over sand dunes with numerous swales or dips in the track surface.

In these circumstances, if you need to carry a large number of jerry cans, it may be best to remove the middle row of seats and build a frame in which the jerry cans can be placed and locked in. This not only ensures that the load on the roof and roof rack is not exceeded, but also keeps the centre of gravity low and may help avoid a roll over situation in sandy country or steep mountainous terrain with eroded tracks. Of course, if carrying fuel inside, you need to ensure that there are absolutely no leaks or spillage (especially with petrol) and under no circumstances should you fill the jerry cans whilst they are inside the vehicle or decant the fuel from the jerry can to the vehicle without removing it first to the open air. This prevents the build up of fuel vapours in the enclosed cabin of the vehicle where a spark from any source could ignite those fumes.

The transfer of fuel from the jerry can to the fuel tank should also be thought through and practised before you leave home. Many filler necks on vehicles, especially unleaded fuel varieties, have a very small fuel filler neck. This is often smaller than the funnel you are using to transfer the fuel, hence more fuel goes down the side of the vehicle than into the tank. The funnel should have a gauze filter and be able to locate inside the filler neck without the need for you to hold it in place.

There are jiggler style siphons available to help siphon fuel from the jerry can to the vehicle. The old method of sucking up fuel through a hose and siphoning it out is not recommended as you are likely to get a mouth full of diesel or petrol that could cause you harm—in a remote location medical help can be a long way away if required.

Be wary of borrowing your mate's jerry cans, whilst this may be a cheap alternative to purchasing your own, their history is unknown. Older steel jerry

cans tend to rust inside or if the jerry can has been used previously to hold water or some other liquid, some of this liquid may remain in the can and pollute your spare fuel supplies. Modern vehicles have high pressure fuel pumps that are very sensitive to pollutants and once your fuel pump becomes contaminated it can lead to the vehicle running with reduced power or not at all. Many modern engine management systems will simply shut down or go into limp mode if they detect a problem with fuel supply. This could be disastrous if you are in a very remote location. Or at least very inconvenient as it can mean a slow journey to the next town with no guarantee that it will have the appropriate gear to repair the fuel filter or reset the computers in the engine management system. Carrying spare fuel filters and knowing where the fuel filter is located is a great idea, even if you have long range fuel tanks.

Finally, wherever you store your jerry cans, you need to ensure they are secure. If in inside the vehicle they should be stored behind a cargo barrier to ensure they do not become missiles in the event of an accident or roll over. Strap them down into a frame using ratchet style straps (never use an elastic style strap often called ockey straps, as these can break when installing them and cause severe damage to your eyes). If using the roof rack for storage of the jerry cans, make sure they are secure. You may need to purchase a jerry can holder from a car parts supplier, for example, Rhino Racks make jerry can holders for their excellent range of roof racks. I suggest using ratchet style straps to keep them in place. Always store the jerry cans upright to avoid any leakage through the pouring lip, and when you fill the jerry can leave some space in the can for expansion in the hot sun to avoid leakage of the fuel. Make sure you test all your jerry cans for leaks and proper storage before you set off on your big trip. One last tip, if storing a number of jerry cans side by side its a good idea to use some marine carpet as a buffer between each jerry can (even the polyurethane type), as this will prevent chafing and the rubbing of holes through the cans on those dusty and corrugated outback roads.

roof racks

Its fair to say that when you head outback there is a lot of extra gear to carry. I've already mentioned some of the items that might end up on a roof rack; spare tyres and jerry cans for example. I've also mentioned that it is vitally important that you are aware of the weight that the vehicle manufacturer recommends for either the roof rails or the gutters (where fitted) that normally support a roof rack. Exceed these recommendations and you will end up having major fatigue problems in your roof rails or gutters.

Before you choose a roof rack you need to determine what it is you will be carrying up there. This will help you determine the size of the rack you require and how heavy duty it needs to be. Remember, if you have an all steel roof rack you may already be nearing the recommended weight for the roof area, add to this a spare tyre

and a couple of jerry cans and suddenly you have exceeded the weight limit.

Apart from the spare wheel and jerry can what else might you want to store on the roof rack? Try to keep the other items as light as possible. Remember to keep the weight down low so as not to compromise your vehicle's centre of gravity. Therefore, stowing light weight equipment on your roof rack, such as your tent and sleeping bags, in a roof top bag is not a bad idea.

In some remote locations you may need to carry your own firewood and the only place to do this is on the roof rack, it avoids all manner of nasty crawling and biting things from invading the interior of your vehicle. So, leaving some space on the roof rack for the firewood isn't a bad idea. See how quickly the size required for a decent roof rack can grow. Even if you think you only need a half or three quarter rack, it is probably worthwhile getting a full length unit, if not only for the purpose of storing some firewood.

DALES GORGE
ROUTE LEVEL 1

3 KM RETURN
2 HRS

Karijini National Park, Pilbara, Western Australia

The most robust roof rack would have to be an all steel version. These are virtually indestructible and if they should show signs of fatigue they can be welded in either a local country town, outback station or, if you are adept at doing some bush welding, beside your remote area camp.

However, if the weight of the roof rack is an issue there are some excellent alloy style racks available from the leading aftermarket suppliers. These units do not lend themselves easily to outback repairs but they are usually quite sufficient for the annual outback trip as opposed to a lifetime of scrub bashing.

There have been many modern versions of roof racks crop up in recent times, models such as the Rhino Rack systems are quite robust and although they require quite a deal of assembling when first installed they have proved their toughness over many outback kilometres.

I have seen many roof racks that just seem to consist of two or three rail type cross bars attached to the roof rails or gutters. These systems are definitely the lower end of the market and whilst they may be great for taking the surf board to the beach or helping your mate move house, they are not really designed for a spare wheel to be carried across a thousand corrugations on the Anne Beadell Highway—and their failure rate in the outback is quite high.

No matter what roof rack system you chose it will consist of some form of nut, bolt and screw system to hold it in place. All of these nuts, bolts and

screws need to be watched carefully whilst on your trip as the vibrations created by off-road driving tend to work them loose. Keep the spanner and socket set handy or the allen keys close by so you can check each nut and bolt at the end of the day's drive. This could save you suddenly seeing your roof rack arrive on your bonnet.

Another worthy tip is to get a roof rack with some form of flooring in it, most steel and alloy units can be optioned up with a mesh floor. The issue is, if you do have to climb up onto the roof rack to load gear, especially firewood which can require some juggling, then you need to ensure that you have a safe footing. If you have a cross rail system it is easy for your foot to slip between the rails then tripping yourself, easily breaking your ankle, or worse, falling head first off the roof rack altogether.

If storing your tent and sleeping gear on the roof rack, I've found it worthwhile to place a large piece of marine carpet between the roof rack and the tent or storage bag, as this prevents chafing on the roof

rack cross bars/mesh floor which can rub through the canvas of your tent and roof storage bag.

The roof rack also allows you to fit an awning to the side of the roof rack, a great option on those hot or wet days. The downside to the roof rack is that it does increase the wind drag effect on the vehicle and will lead to increased fuel consumption and some wind noise. But the biggest deficit to a roof rack is that once fitted you will find it difficult to enter undercover car parks due to the overall height of the vehicle being increased. You may even be unable to use your own garage at home. Look before you enter, it wouldn't be the first time a roof rack has been wiped off by a supermarket car park!

roof rack storage bags/pods

I touched on these in the Roof Rack section. There are a number of excellent canvas, heavy duty vinyl and fibreglass storage pods on the market these days. These are ideal for carrying soft items such as sleeping bags, air beds and clothes bags. These items are relatively light and lend themselves to storage on the roof rack. The material bags, such as canvas or vinyl, provide a level of protection unequalled by the commonly seen flapping blue tarp. Most storage bags come with tie down hooks, although I also recommend throwing a couple of ratchet style straps across the bag to prevent it moving around too vigorously which may lead to excessive wear on the tie down points. It is best to get a bag that can be opened on three sides so you can throw the top cover back to aid loading and

unloading. As mentioned previously, place a piece of marine carpet between the storage bag and the roof rack to prevent chaffing. The fibreglass storage pods are becoming more popular, these provide both a dry and dust free storage space, plus an aerodynamic effect that aids fuel consumption.

storage systems/cargo barriers

Now we move inside the vehicle to offer some ideas on how to make your outback trip more comfortable. The number one item here is the humble storage system. If you are one of those people that simply throw all the gear in the back of the four-wheel drive, then you will know what a jumbled mess it can be. No matter how carefully you pack all that gear in the rear storage area, every time you stop, the one item you want has always worked its way to the bottom of the pile. Your holiday becomes more of a nightmare; searching, packing and unpacking and eventually losing your temper not only with the junk but with your travelling partner—not a happy camper at all.

The answer is so simple—just organise it. The best way to organise it is to put it into compartments. Even if you don't invest in a manufactured storage system simply placing similar items into plastic containers will make your life easier. But the best suggestion is to either build your own storage system or shell out some hard earned dollars on what will become your best investment.

The first step is to establish what it is you are going to store in the back of the vehicle. You may even need to take a couple of weekend camping trips just to see what you require and how it needs to be packed. Once you know what you want to put in the rear of the vehicle, have worked out the items you use most frequently and those that are there just in case, then you can design your storage system.

As mentioned there are some excellent storage systems available and whilst they come in fairly standard configurations, any supplier worth his salt will be happy to design one to suit your needs. I've been using an Off Road Systems storage unit in the rear of my Landcruiser for over nine years now and I can assure you it has been all over Australia, and its never given me an ounce of trouble.

The beauty of an integrated storage system is that it makes excellent use of all of the space available. These units generally go between the rear door and the back of the second row of seats. It may require removal of the third row of seats if fitted, which in some states if you read the motor registry regulations, may actually be unlawful. However, I have not personally known of anyone that has had registration of their motor vehicle denied because they had a storage system in place.

I am a great believer in having a cargo barrier installed in your four-wheel drive, this ideally goes behind the second row of seats just before the storage system. If you have ever seen what happens to a four-wheel drive and its contents when it rolls over at speed on a country road, you will like me, forever agree that cargo barriers

should always be fitted. They do save lives, simple as that!

With the cargo barrier in place, you can now effectively use all of the storage space from the floor of the rear compartment up to the roof lining. The storage system will help you do this in an efficient manner.

In your planning for storage of items in the rear of the vehicle you will have established that you need to carry an amount of vehicle recovery gear. This equipment can be quite heavy and due to its rugged nature tends to knock other things around that it is stored with. It also needs to be accessed quickly if needed, hopefully it is not required too often, and the recovery gear can become covered in mud and be wet after use. So there are a lot of reasons to keep it away from your egg container, or anything else for that matter.

Therefore it needs its own cubby hole down low in the vehicle. There is no better location than an enclosed drawer on the bottom of the storage system, this way it is accessible only when needed and keeps the heavy, wet, muddy gear isolated from everything else.

You will also have established that you will need man's best friend, the humble car fridge. For ease of accessing it, keep the fridge as low as possible in the rear of the vehicle and put it on a slide base with a spring base to absorb the vibrations. Ideally the fridge goes next to the recovery drawer across the rear of the storage compartment. The space above the drawer and the fridge can be put to good use too, further drawers or simple storage units that hold plastic containers are ideal.

A well designed storage system allows you to carry a heap of gear that is always easily accessible. Those little nooks and crannies toward the rear of the storage unit can include your box of spare parts, tools and vehicle jack, the things that you are not likely to use too often but if you do, they can be accessed with a minimum of fuss. It's even possible for these storage systems to include slide out tables, over head lights and a top shelf which still allows items to be stored right up to the roof lining and anchored in place.

Think about use of the rear luggage area whilst camping, especially at night. Have your favourite four-wheel drive workshop install some extra camp lights in the rear of the vehicle to light up your fridge, food preparation area and storage system.

Whilst at the workshop get a couple of heavy duty power outlets installed in the rear of the vehicle wired directly from the second battery with their own in-line fuse. This will take care of the fridge, an inverter, which I'll cover shortly and power leads for external camp lights. Suddenly, the back of the four-wheel drive is becoming a very nice place to be.

power supplies

So now we are starting to get the four-wheel drive set-up fairly nicely for your outback journey. These days there is a lot of great gear to make your outback trip quite comfortable. From the cool fridge, to extra lighting, radio and navigational equipment, even hot showers. But before you get too deeply involved in adding all this gear, we need to offer some advice on how to power it all.

dual battery management system

Gammon Ranges, South Australia

It is fairly obvious that you can easily set-up your vehicle with all the modern conveniences of home. Unfortunately they all require a power supply and when you are remote area camping the only reliable power source will be the battery in your vehicle. Never lose sight of what the main purpose is of your vehicle's battery—to start the vehicle each time you turn the ignition key or hit the start engine button. If this does nothing, then none of your modern conveniences are going to work either and their importance suddenly pales to insignificance as the reality hits home of your real predicament.

Fortunately, the aftermarket four-wheel drive world thought of this possibility also. The most common method of ensuring that you have sufficient power for everything (especially to start the vehicle) is the installation of a second battery. This second battery is usually a deep cycle unit which is designed to be continually drained of all life and then recharged. Your standard starting battery does not like being treated in this fashion.

The deep cycle or second battery's primary purpose is to run all your accessories such as UHF radio, fridge, camp lights, inverters, DVD players etc. This leaves your main starter battery to simply take care of one very important task—the task of getting your engine ticking over each morning.

However, unless you have the second battery installed correctly and isolated from the main battery you may easily find yourself with two flat batteries in the morning whilst camped at Durba Springs on the Canning Stock Route. So the next most important lesson here is to ensure that a qualified four-wheel drive workshop that knows what is required of a second battery in a four-wheel drive does the installation for you. All too frequent I've seen incorrect installations performed by "My mate's an auto electrician, so I got him to do it". Note that the person doing the work has to know that the second battery is there to power all the extra accessories (except the electric winch which must be powered by the main battery) and that it needs the appropriate wiring, isolation from the main battery and charging sequence (the main battery should always be charged before the second battery).

The deep cycle battery will usually be installed under the bonnet, but many modern four-wheel drives have limited space in the engine bay. This is where the good mechanic is sorted out from the best mechanics. Once again, an experienced four-wheel drive workshop will know how to relocate items under the bonnet to get the extra battery in or, if necessary know where to locate the extra battery elsewhere in the vehicle if required. Many people are staggered to learn that their extra battery may cost well in excess of $800 often thinking that an extra battery should only be around $150. They forget that the installation requires an extra battery cradle, isolator, lengths of appropriate cabling and a few hours of installation especially if it's not straight forward. But this is money well spent and you can rest easy that your main battery will have sufficient life in it in the morning to get you back on the road.

a second battery has many uses

self-sufficient touring set-up

Portable battery chargers are available but these take up space in the rear of the vehicle and take time and a power source of their own to get your battery charged sufficiently to start the vehicle. With diesel powered motor vehicles the cranking power required to turn over the high compression diesel motor is very high and many portable chargers or battery packs don't have sufficient grunt to handle a diesel motor.

Many caravan owners have equipped themselves with solar panels to put charge back into their batteries. Whilst this is an ideal power source for people stopping in one location for an extended period, if your travels are limited to short treks away or you are constantly on the move you may find that the solar panel concept struggles to deliver sufficient power output for your needs. Be aware that if using solar panels they do require a clear and direct view of the sun for most of the day, even the slightest shadow from a tree branch can cause a drastic power drop. The solar panel also needs appropriate wiring between the panel and the battery, especially if any distance is involved as voltage drop can be to such an extent that your battery does not become fully charged even after an extended period. If going down this path, it is best to speak with some experts; people who actually use the gear, a great source for this info will be websites such as www.exploroz.com.au

The humble inverter is something that all travellers should have stored in their vehicle. This small piece of equipment is ideal for converting your 12 volt power from your car battery to 240 volt power

whilst out in the bush. I use my inverter whilst on extended remote area trips to maintain the battery charge in my digital camera, video camera, satellite phone, mobile phone and even my laptop. The current draw for these items is minimal and I'm using my deep cycle battery anyway.

You can acquire larger inverters that will drive electric tools such as grinders and drills and I've even seen a standard home microwave carried in the tray of a Nissan Navara with a large inverter providing the power conversion from a second battery, I wouldn't recommend this application for extended outback trips. But it seemed to work OK for a weekend trip.

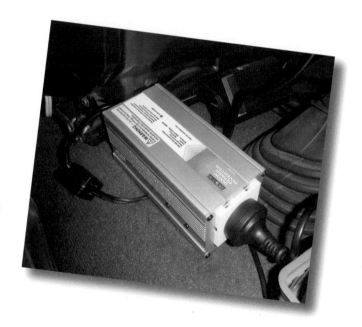

lights

When setting up your vehicle for an outback trip there are two different types of lights to consider. Lights for driving and lights for camping.

I'm often asked "I don't intend to do any driving at night, so do I really need driving lights?" I have a couple of stock answers, but the best one I use is to relate a true story that happened to me recently. There I was cut off by the Paroo River in flood at Eulo. It was just on dusk and although I had been driving all day, and dearly wanted to make camp and throw the swag down, I had to keep driving for another three hours into the night to cross the dry Paroo crossing at Hungerford. If I hadn't, by morning that road too would have been cut and I would have been faced with a 600 kilometre round trip to get to the other side of the river. I was very glad to have a good set of driving lights that night!

There is an enormous range of driving lights on the market these days and you can spend anywhere from a few hundred dollars to in excess of a thousand dollars. In my opinion, such an exorbitant outlay is overkill. There are some top quality lights on the market for a few hundred dollars that do the job very well. The critical thing I find with driving lights is keeping them on the front of the vehicle, and I'm not just referring to the light fingered people in cities who seem to want to borrow your hard earned gear. I've seen way too many driving lights break off at the mounting bracket on our outback corrugated roads. I've found that the big heavy robust looking lights and brackets aren't

always the strongest when it comes to withstanding metal fatigue caused by constant vibration. For example take a look at the driving lights on my Landcruiser, they are big and provide fantastic light at night and yet they have been across and around Australia several times and never shown any signs of fatigue. Their brackets and mounts look decidedly flimsy and yet the light is rock solid, just perfect for outback travel. Having a pencil beam and one spread beam is a good combination as it helps to illuminate the road ahead as well as off to the side where you might spot a kangaroo lurking.

Alternatively, you can get some great upgrades for your standard low and high beam. This will overcome the problem of the driving lights disappearing off the front of the vehicle for one reason or another.

In camp, for example when I finally crossed the Paroo near Hungerford at 10pm and it was time to throw the swag down, I like the ease of use offered by a fluoro light. The light is plugged into the extra power outlet I have installed in the rear of my vehicle, which is powered off my deep cycle battery. The fluoro light throws a good white light which easily provides sufficient light around the vehicle for making camp and the power drain on the deep cycle battery is virtually negligible. Most camp fluoro lights are supplied with at least seven metres of lead which allows you to run the light off the battery or power outlet all the way into your tent. The real beauty of the fluoro light is that it generates no heat or sound, compare this to the traditional gas lantern seen around campsites. These traditional gas lanterns are a source of extreme heat and the constant hiss of gas burning

to accompany you through the night is rather annoying compared to the silent operation of a fluoro light.

If you've ever used a gas lantern you will also know that the mantle will always require replacement at the most inconvenient of times; such as when making camp in the dark or just as dinner is to be served. The fluoro light wins hands down for convenience and longevity and there is no extra power source such as gas or petrol required, its all there, under your bonnet in the form of your deep cycle battery.

There are many other forms of camp lights available such as battery powered units and rechargeable battery powered lanterns, whilst these avoid the heat and noise of a gas or petrol lantern the batteries do tend to fail at the most inconvenient time, and they are extra weight in an already overloaded vehicle. I still support the fluoro camp light as the best option.

all the comforts of home

There really is no excuse to go without the comforts of home on your next four-wheel drive trip. You can even have a hot shower in the middle of nowhere. Shower units for camping come in a variety of forms, from the humble hang the bag of water in the sun until it heats up, to a fully integrated heat conversion kit on the vehicle's engine cooling system. These integrated shower units may cost a few hundred dollars, but again, if you are going to be away from basic facilities for a while, nothing beats having a hot shower at the end of the day.

The integrated systems are available from good four-wheel drive accessory outlets and consist of the heat exchange unit which plumbs into the vehicle's existing heater system, a small pump, the necessary piping for intake of water from a bucket or water container, and outlet piping usually via a hand held shower rose. Add to this one of the quick and easy to erect pop up shower tents and a car mat or rubberised door mat for the floor to keep the mud and sand away and you have an instant shower recess no matter where you are. You soon learn that you can have a very comforting hot shower in less than 10 litres of water.

spare parts

Now that you have your vehicle well set-up for its outback travel its time to think about the 'what if'. Carrying a few basic spare parts is a great idea, but don't be concerned if you don't think you have a clue on how to change a fan belt or a fuel filter. Let me put it this way, if you don't have it then nothing other than a tow truck and a lot of money is going to help, but if you've got a replacement for the errant part someone else may come along who is happy to help out—probably just for a shout at the next pub.

The modern vehicles of today don't lend themselves too well to backyard mechanics, but you should still carry what I term a first aid kit for your vehicle. This will include those items that if they fail or malfunction will stop the vehicle in its tracks, and yet they can be replaced by most people. I suggest having a box (read plastic container) for these parts which is stored in one of those nooks or crannies that will exist at the rear of the storage system near the cargo barrier. In this box have; a set of fan belts including drive belts and air conditioning belts, a fuel filter (if your vehicle has an in-line filter), a spare air filter, and if your vehicle is more than five years old replacement upper and lower radiator hoses. Add to this an assortment of fuses to not only fit those in the vehicle but also the accessories you have, including communication gear (UHF, HF or satellite phones), fridge, inverters and lights if they rely on a fuse system, put in a fuse puller too for the vehicle mounted fuses. Now add to this some engine oil, differential oil and transmission oil if it is not a sealed unit, and finally carry a litre of brake fluid just in case.

vehicle recovery equipment

The amount of vehicle recovery gear that you carry will depend largely on where you intend to travel and whether this travel will be alone or in a group. Naturally, if you are travelling alone and into isolated areas, then you need to be as self-sufficient as possible.

But first I need to define the word isolated, as many people will read this as being some huge off the beaten track excursion across a trackless desert where no person has driven previously. Whilst this is isolated, I also class some of the four-wheel drive tracks only a couple of hours from our major capital cities as potentially isolated. So, what makes a track or place isolated? For my reckoning isolated is any place where others are not likely to pass within a 24 hour period. Or one where you would not be able to raise help within a two hour period and this help can physically reach you in no more than two more hours.

For example if you are stuck at the bottom of a greasy, muddy fire trail and no-one is likely to pass this way in the next 24 hours, or if you were to try to walk out to get help but could not guarantee finding someone within two hours of leaving your vehicle, then this is an isolated place.

The reasoning behind these times is that 24 hours with your car in extreme heat or cold without food or water is about the most a healthy adult or child can withstand. Or walking in extreme heat or cold for approximately two hours without finding assistance is roughly the point where heat exhaustion or hypothermia will start to take effect.

If being stuck at the bottom of a muddy slope in the Blue Mountains could result in your demise then having some vehicle recovery gear is a small price to pay. If being stuck in a boggy salt pan halfway between Well 16 and the Calvert Range in Western Australia on your own could be fixed by having equipped yourself with some recovery gear, then why wouldn't you? Most people reading this book are likely to be travelling with their partner or family, putting their lives at risk just to save a few dollars on recovery gear, simply makes no sense at

all. The last thing I want to do is to encourage you to head out bush without thinking about the term 'what if'. My policy is to always apply the 'what if' question, and if I don't have an answer then simply I shouldn't be placing myself or my family in this risky situation.

Even if you are travelling with others, you need to think about the 'what if' and still apply the time frames described above. If your companions can't get help within these time periods then you are still at major risk in the worse case scenario.

The best thing about vehicle recovery gear is it is cost effective. For $1000 you can have everything you need in terms of vehicle recovery gear. A very small price to pay when compared to the cost of your four-wheel drive, camper trailer or caravan, and the value you place on yourself, your partner and your family.

If travelling alone you should have the following recovery gear stored in your four-wheel drive.

- Hand winch, of at least 1.6 ton lifting capacity
- 2 snatch or pulley blocks
- 20 or 30 metre winch strap extension
- 2 tree protectors
- 3 metre length of drag chain
- Bridle strap
- 4 x 3¼ ton rated shackles
- 2 x 4¾ ton rated shackles
- 9 metre 8 ton snatch recovery strap (If in sand dune country a 20 metre 8 ton snatch strap also)
- Leather gloves
- Exhaust jack
- Sand mats
- Axe
- Shovel
- Bush Saw

If travelling in a group then the above gear could be divided between the group, but each vehicle should carry its own snatch recovery strap and two shackles of 3¼ ton rating.

It is imperative that your vehicle is fitted with appropriate vehicle recovery points both at the front and rear of the vehicle. Not all vehicles have these recovery points fitted when purchased new, and some have them removed when the dealer fits that nice shiny bull bar. So it is best to talk to a dedicated four-wheel drive accessory or repair workshop about the quality of your recovery points and the fitting of appropriate recovery points where necessary. Never use a tie down or transport hook, tow ball, bull bar, or any other non recovery rated point on your vehicle. Incorrect use of this equipment can lead to serious injury or death.

I highly recommend you carry my book 4WD Driving Skills - A Manual for On and Off Road Driving (CSIRO Publishing, 2001) which explains how to use and set-up the above recovery gear as well as all the necessary four-wheel driving tips.

wet track in outback Queensland

chapter 3

OFF-ROAD CAMPER TRAILERS & OFF-ROAD CARAVANS

off-road camper trailers

There has been an explosion in the number of camper trailers available to the outback traveller in recent years. A visit to any caravan and camping show will soon bombard you with multiple choices and huge claims by the various manufacturers. So what should the prospective camper trailer purchaser look for when choosing their trailer?

Firstly, let's examine why people purchase a trailer. It seems to me there are a variety of reasons given but the most common relate to:

- The family don't like sleeping on the ground in a tent.
- There isn't enough room in the four-wheel drive for all the camping gear.
- The family prefers a bit more luxury than that supplied by tent camping.
- We want something quick to set up and dismantle.

As you see these all relate to perceived pitfalls in the use of the usual camping gear, such as a tent, sleeping bags and cooking gear.

With the huge variety of camper trailers on the market, choosing a camper trailer that is best suited to your needs becomes quite difficult. The best thing to do is prepare a check list of your requirements; some of those items on the check list might include the following:

- What type of touring are you going to do; only sealed roads, some unsealed road or maybe full on four-wheel drive adventures?
- What is the weight of the trailer and what can your vehicle legally and easily tow?
- How many people in your family need to be accommodated in the trailer?
- How much gear will you be storing in the trailer?
- Do you prefer cooking quarters inside or outside?
- How easy is the trailer to erect and disassemble?
- What is the track record of the trailer you are considering?
- How much money do you wish to spend?

Now let's look at each question in more detail.

what type of touring are you going to do, only sealed roads, some unsealed road or maybe full on four wheel drive adventures?

This is possibly the most important question as it will dictate the size, weight, construction and cost of the trailer you are after. For example if you are only planning on doing the big lap of Australia without leaving a sealed road, then your choice of trailer actually becomes much easier and cheaper. Robust construction and therefore the usual accompanying high cost are no longer a priority. However, if you are going to explore every nook and cranny of Australia, intend to go off-road with it as much as possible and drag it behind you anywhere and everywhere, then you need to choose a trailer with real serious off-road capability. If your needs lay somewhere in-between, don't be fooled into thinking you can purchase an off-road trailer with some big white wheels that the dealer calls 'the off-road pack'. Because if you still intend to drag the trailer across the Gibb River Road, even if it is only once, you don't want it falling apart on you.

what is the weight of the trailer and what can your vehicle legally and easily tow?

You should answer the second question first, even before you start looking for a trailer, no point getting your heart set on a particular model if your vehicle is never going to be able to tow

it. Also, don't push your vehicle's limits, if the unladen weight of the trailer is approaching the legal tow limit of the vehicle, then you will find it will struggle once the trailer is loaded. You need to know that any off-road work using a heavy trailer is going to seriously compromise your vehicle's ability. In soft sand the trailer will be like an anchor, and on steep inclines, what the vehicle easily climbed without the trailer may become impossible with the trailer hooked up.

how many people in your family need to be accommodated in the trailer?

All too often the reason given for choosing a trailer is to safely accommodate the family away from the crawlies and bugs. Yet, most off-road trailers have fold out canvas sections. Any additional persons above the first two will find they are sleeping in this fold out section. Sure, mum and dad have a double bed off the ground on top of the trailer; but the kids are still down on the canvas floor, on their air beds, on the ground where the perceived creepy crawlies are found. This tends to destroy the argument for the trailer to some degree. There are few off-road trailers that will accommodate an average size family off the ground. Also, the sizing of some trailers is a bit like the sizing of tents, most two man tents accommodate one person comfortably; the extra person usually takes up any storage requirements created by the first person. So a four person camper trailer is likely to have a double bed on top of the trailer and space for either their luggage or cooking gear in the fold out section, or the kids air beds or stretchers—but not both. That's why you see so many trailers with zip on annexes. But all these zip on bits take time to erect, and most quoted set up times never include the zip on extras (which usually cost more), and the zip bits rarely have floors, so whoever is in this section cooking or relaxing is on the ground with all the creepy crawlies you were trying to get away from.

how much gear will you be storing in the trailer?

This is a really important question as all too often the new purchaser gets all excited with the shiny new model in the showroom which is totally bereft of any real living essentials. Once you start to load up the trailer suddenly you find all that space you had has disappeared. Secondly the weight of the trailer has now sky

rocketed. If this means you will still store all the gear in the four-wheel drive, then why have all this added weight on the back? Like planning your outback trip, you need to sit down and prepare a list of all the items you will carry and then, in your minds eye, carefully plot where it will all go in the trailer and imagine what the end result will look like, how you will live with it and how much it all weighs.

do you prefer cooking quarters inside or outside?

For every person I have spoken to that prefers to have their cooking quarters outside of the main body of their camp trailer I have spoken to an equal number that prefer it inside. My advice is to once again imagine exactly what it will be like to cook dinner for you and your family no matter where the cooking equipment is located. If inside, how much heat and fumes are generated and how quickly can they be dispersed—nothing worse than having your bedding and everything else you own smelling of last week's seafood barbecue. What about space inside the trailer if the stove is in there too, is there room to move around; what if it's raining outside and the rest of the family want to huddle in the trailer, how much space is there now? Alternatively if you have chosen an outside cooking space how does it work if its raining, how long does it take to erect a zip on awning over the cooking area, is there an increased fire risk if outside or under an awning, will you feel part of the family or will they be inside watching the television whilst you prepare dinner, how cold in

Bramwell Junction, Cape York

winter will it be outside, what about the flies in summer? See, and you thought choosing a trailer would be easy.

how easy is the trailer to erect and disassemble?

This is another reason some people choose a trailer over a tent. At the four-wheel drive show the guy selling it had it up in 30 seconds and down in the same time, but the best you have ever done was 15 minutes! Sound familiar? That's because when you are erecting your trailer you are doing so to its full and final completion; ready to cook in, occupy and rest. It's all the little things that have to be connected, set-up and repositioned that you don't see demonstrated in the 30 second display. Also, remember, you will be doing this in all manner of weather conditions from bright hot sunshine to cold wet weather, and all this adds to the set-up time. Who cares if it takes 45 minutes each evening and each morning to make your life simple. What?

May I suggest, don't just take the salesperson's advice, have a go yourself. He is practised in the operation, you might find it takes two of you to lift the weight, swing the cover over the trailer and squeeze it altogether to get the locking tabs to close properly. Imagine what its like outside of the showroom in the wind and rain, how easy is the erection process then? What about all those add on bits that are essential; is setting up your ideal camp taking close to 30 minutes now? That is about 15 minutes too long. Trust me; if you are on an extended outback trip and it takes longer than 15 minutes to set-up camp, then you have the wrong gear.

what is the track record of the trailer you are considering?

This is a very important question if you are choosing a trailer to go off-road or up the Birdsville Track. Don't take the salesperson's word for it, what do you think they are going to tell you—of course it's the next best thing since elastic sided boots. You need to talk to some owners of the trailer; sure the salesperson will have a list of them, but get onto some of the forum sites and ask the question. Take a look at www.exploroz.com.au and the questions asked of trailers in their forum section, and suddenly you start to see some real world use and feedback. This is part of your research way before you go to the showroom. When you do get there be armed with questions; ask what the warranty is like, what happens if something breaks at Oodnadatta, if you've read of numerous common problems and the dealer says, "never heard of that breaking" walk away, he or she can't be trusted.

how much money do you wish to spend?

Whoops! Should have asked this question first. Did you know you can purchase a camper trailer for as little as $10 000 or as much as $75 000+! So if you only have $20 000 to spend then there's not much point looking at anything more expensive. Unless of course you buy second hand, which isn't such a bad

Bush camp along the Plenty Highway, Northern Territory

idea, there are lots of camper trailers that have done their one big trip and then their owners have moved on. Again, be realistic with your budget and stick to it, and don't forget to include some extra dollars as you will inevitably be talked into some extras.

You might say that I have not painted a great picture for the purchase of an off-road trailer, and I have to admit I'm not a big fan of some trailers. They can be, just an excessively, expensive tent on wheels that restricts you from exploring Australia. But, having said that, I have taken plenty of top class trailers on various outback tracks which have performed faultlessly. The greatest mistake people make when choosing an off-road trailer is not purchasing one suitable to their particular requirements; this is especially the case with those wanting to explore the remote tracks of Australia. If you think you can do that on the cheap, I'm afraid you are going to be very disappointed, sooner or later.

A couple of things to consider when purchasing you're off road trailer:

- Ensure that the trailer's wheels are the same size as those fitted to your tow vehicle; this saves on the need to carry extra spare tyres and allows easy interchange of the tyres, which will ultimately save you money.
- Ensure that the track of the trailer (the width of the axle between the wheels) is the same as that of the tow vehicle. This makes towing in an off-road situation easier, especially when in soft ground like sand or mud, as the tyres on the trailer can follow the wheel tracks made by the vehicle's wheels.
- A longer draw bar aids in manoeuvring the trailer, especially reversing. However, a draw bar that is too long may come into contact with irregularities in the track surface (such as conservation mounds) and strand the vehicle.
- A tow hitch that provides flexibility—both to each side and up and down is essential if you are going to tow your trailer into rough terrain. Without this flexibility the tow ball mount can be damaged, the vehicle may have its rear wheels forced off the ground, or permanent damage occur to the draw bar.
- Be aware that the added weight of the trailer may require you to add heavy duty suspension or air bags to the rear of your vehicle. Leave this unaddressed and at worst your vehicle will be uncontrollable and at the least your vehicle's headlights, which are pointing skyward, will annoy every other driver.

camper trailer driver training

An off-road trailer will require some additional driving skills. There are a number of commercial off-road trailer courses available, for example my own company, Great Divide Tours offers these. An off-road trailer course will demonstrate the skill required to tow a trailer in an off-road situation; it will demonstrate that, no matter what trailer or vehicle is involved, the added weight and length does substantially restrict the off-road capability of your vehicle. You will find that the trailer is difficult to tow in soft sand, especially up and down sand dunes, and that on steep inclines the climbing ability of the vehicle is restricted.

Changing weather conditions have a greater effect on vehicles towing off-road trailers. For example imagine a steep, slippery climb and the loss of traction; reversing back down with your trailer in tow suddenly becomes a very difficult exercise as the trailer tries to jackknife. On a steep, slippery climb it may be impossible to move forward to correct the jackknifing trailer, so using your winch gear to straighten your vehicle and trailer may be your only option. Similarly, on outback roads such as the Birdsville Track, once they receive some rain the road can become extremely slippery and towing a trailer in these conditions can be very difficult. Also, many regional councils may close their roads to heavy vehicles when wet, although they may allow four-wheel drive access, the fine print says once you fit a trailer you are classed as a heavy vehicle.

If you are in the market for an off-road trailer, my best advice is to try before you buy. Many of the

major companies will have units available for hire. I strongly suggest you spend a few dollars and hire a trailer for at least a couple of days to allow you some time with it to see how it best suits your needs. If you are planning a once in a lifetime trip, either consider hiring a good off-road trailer or establishing with the company if they have a purchase and buy back scheme. Many of the better companies offer this and you will be surprised how little this may actually cost you. For example try Ultimate Campers and Kimberley Kampers for this option.

Generally speaking your camper trailer should be equipped with springs and shock absorbers in its suspension if you are going to take it off the sealed road, and you still need to carry spare shocks for it. Also, establish what servicing is required of the wheel bearings and carry the necessary spares with you to perform this whilst away. Finally, establish what the warranty is and how it can be enacted if you are halfway down the west coast of Western Australia.

off-road caravans

There has also been a surge in the popularity of this style of caravan. Much of what I have said about the camper trailer is applicable to the off-road caravan. In my opinion the major issues with off-road caravans include:

- Their cost – often in excess of $100 000.
- Their size – length, breadth and height, which can severely restrict where you can tow them in some off-road areas.
- Their weight – these vans are heavy and thus they need a big heavy vehicle to successfully tow them. This weight also means they will not be good in sandy country or steep hills found on fire trails.

For a touring set-up for a 12 month trip around Australia, with the ability to handle roads such as the Oodnadatta Track, Gibb River Road and Birdsville Track, they are a great option. But, don't expect to take one into Purnululu National Park (the sign at the turn off on the highway says NO!); or up Cape York despite what you might see on some DVD's.

chapter 4

COMMUNICATION EQUIPMENT

what is it and do you need it?

I'm almost loath to write anything about this subject because it is changing so quickly. It is probably the most exciting aspect of outback travel and the plethora of different communication formats available is just outstanding. However, let me try to explain what is out there and what you may or may not require depending on your individual needs.

Communications equipment has two broad categories, the first, voice communications allowing you to stay in contact with fellow travelling companions and people at home or not in your travelling group. Generally this equipment includes two-way radio equipment and satellite telephones. The second category is related to mapping and the identification of your location whilst out and about. This includes Global Positioning Systems (GPS) and Emergency Position Indicating Radio Beacon (EPIRB). So let me look at each type of communication equipment and explain what it is, which may help you determine if you need this type of gear.

cb (citizen band) radio

In days gone by when Smokey was trying to stop a Convoy (you need to be a certain age to remember the CW McCall song of 1975) CB radio was the choice of communication by truckies and outback travellers alike. This provided two-way radio communication between vehicles on the road and in the bush. Its voice quality was questionable and its range limited to a few kilometres at best; although certain atmospheric conditions allowed

road train

side band radio waves to be used and at times your message could be heard over vast distances (this was known as skip—as the radio signal skipped or bounced off the ionosphere). But CB radio is almost dead these days, being replaced by UHF radio.

uhf (ultra high frequency) radio

This is definitely the two-way radio of choice by most outback travellers. Truckies use it, caravan owners, four-wheel drivers, road crews, building sites, the list goes on and on. A UHF radio will provide communications between anyone with a UHF radio using the same channel. It provides very clear voice reproduction. The performance of a

UHF radio is affected by landforms, aerial size and power output.

Landforms affect the radio broadcast, as the signal issued, when you speak into the microphone, travels in a straight line from the aerial so if there is a hill between you and the receiving radio, the message does not pass through the hill.

The location and size of the aerial also affects the radio signal transmission. The taller the aerial the more chance there is of getting your signal out and it travelling further. Therefore an ideal aerial is one that is two metres high located in the centre of the roof of the four-wheel drive or campervan. The roof of the vehicle can act as what is known as a ground plane, and helps to maintain the power of the signal. However, it is not always appropriate to have your aerial in the centre of the roof as most outback travel vehicles will have a roof rack fitted, and the overall height of the aerial places it in jeopardy of being snapped off by low branches, car ports or even service station awnings. For this reason the most common place to locate a large UHF aerial is on the bull bar of the vehicle. The bonnet acts as the ground plane, but given that the bonnet is behind the aerial the signal strength will be at its greatest going to the rear of the vehicle. Therefore, cars following you may hear your transmissions better than vehicles that are in front of you.

Of course, it is not always possible to have a two metre tall aerial on your vehicle or for that matter on a handheld radio. Many handheld radios come with an aerial that is only up to 100mm in length.

Obviously this radio will not broadcast its signal as far as a vehicle mounted two metre tall aerial.

The power output of the UHF radio will vary between half a watt and five watts. You are unable to purchase anything above five watts in the UHF range of radios. Power again dictates the signal strength so a five watt unit will always outperform a radio with anything less. My experience is that five watt handheld units used in a convoy situation will have a range of about two kilometres at best, where as a half watt radio might only broadcast for 100 metres or less.

UHF radio

The ideal situation is to have a five watt UHF radio fitted into your vehicle with an external aerial mounted on the bull bar with a height ranging between one to two metres. Handheld units may be used as transportable units when out checking the track ahead and giving instructions to the driver as the driver follows your directions over rough ground.

Although most outback cattle and sheep stations use UHF radio for communicating with their employees you can not rely on being able to contact them via the UHF radio if you need help or advice. The UHF radio also has a network of radio repeater stations that allow you to speak over longer distances. There are printed brochures available showing the location and channel number of these repeater stations, these are available from most local country Information Centres or just Google UHF Radio Repeater Stations and you will find numerous sites dedicated to providing this information, such as www.cbradioaustralia.com.au which provides excellent advice on communications equipment.

I would strongly recommend anyone planning an outback trip to have a UHF radio fitted to their vehicle with an external aerial (it's a good idea to carry a spare aerial as they can become damaged by over hanging trees or the constant vibration of corrugated roads). This is almost mandatory if travelling with friends, in a convoy or an organised tag-along tour. Inter-car communication is made so simple and is part of the enjoyment of outback travel. However, even if travelling on your own, you should have a UHF radio with external aerial fitted to your vehicle. You can gain valuable road condition information from other passing motorists, and if on an extended trip you are almost certain to meet other travellers, even spend some time travelling with them, and being able to communicate whilst travelling is essential.

hf (high frequency) radio

The HF Radio is best known for its use with the Royal Flying Doctor Service and was known as RFDS radio. This is a two-way radio system that provides communication capability across vast distances. Primarily the radio is similar to any other CB or UHF radio except it is far more powerful. Prior to the inception of satellite telephones, the HF Radio provided the only means of reliable communication in isolated areas.

Today with the advent of satellite telephones and improved UHF repeater services the HF Radio is not as widely used however, it still provides a vital and useful service.

In recent years the Australian National 4WD Radio Network, which uses HF radio as its means of communication, has grown in presence and offers an excellent service for users of HF radios. It provides position reporting, weather reports on a scheduled daily basis, road condition reports and a message handling service for its members. If you are keen to learn more about HF Radio and the Australian 4WD Radio Network I urge you to visit their website at www.vks737.on.net

The HF Radio can provide an excellent means of keeping in touch with other HF Radio users, or even loved ones at home via the messaging service or the radio telephone call service that it provides. It is certainly worth learning more about the services it provides and comparing its cost and serviceability with other means of communication (namely satellite telephones). The HF Radio's greatest pitfall

reliable communications are an outback essential

is the quality of voice service at times, and the fact it is a two-way radio system which means that only one person can talk at any one time. People who are familiar with two-way radio use don't find this a problem, but others who may rarely use a two-way radio tend to struggle with the requirement of one person speaking and concluding their message with the word 'over' before the other party can respond.

satellite telephones

Twenty years ago this equipment virtually did not exist, but with the advancement in communications of all types, it was inevitable that satellite technology would impact on our ability to communicate with each other.

Firstly, let me state that a satellite telephone is not a replacement for a two-way radio system (UHF or HF). The satellite telephone allows you to talk to anyone who has access to a normal landline telephone, mobile phone or another satellite telephone. But it does this at a cost that is not inconsiderable. A UHF radio allows you to talk to another UHF radio within its short range, free of cost (after the initial purchase price), therefore the satellite telephone does not replace the UHF radio for convoy or car to car communication.

What the satellite telephone does do is almost guarantee, that no matter where you are, you are able to make a connection with the outside world. This may be for the purpose of seeking medical help, gathering advice on a mechanical issue with your vehicle, making a booking at an accommodation

facility or just keeping in touch with family and colleagues.

There are several providers of satellite telephones on the market including Telstra (Iridium) and Globalstar (Pivotel). You can either purchase outright or hire the satellite telephone, there are many outlets that provide one or the other; or both services. I suggest you look at the satellite telephone section on the website www.exploroz.com.au for all the details on satellite telephones and for hiring purposes look at www.landwide.com.au

The downside to this technology is the cost; the equipment costing up to $2000 and the call costs dependent on the telephone use plan you have purchased. A word of warning, don't treat your satellite telephone like a normal mobile or landline telephone, as it can cost you a lot of money for extended and frequent calls. Also, the service can be a little vague locking onto and holding a satellite; and the voice quality can vary, especially with some units that have a distinct delay caused by the use of high orbit satellites. It is best to do a lot of research before spending your dollars.

Having said this, I don't believe anyone should venture into remote areas without a satellite telephone at the ready to seek help if required.

mobile phones

Most people have a mobile phone these days, and whilst they are often quoted as providing service to '97% of the population', the small print says 'over 6% of the Australian mainland'. The problem is that most of your outback travel will be in the 94% of land where there is no mobile coverage. Simply put, don't rely on your mobile phone for communication purposes in outback Australia (and outback can even be just two hours from a major city).

personal locating beacon (plb) and emergency position indicating radio beacon (epirb)

These two devices are similar—they provide an emergency signal service in the event you are in a life threatening situation. The PLB is used primarily on land and the EPIRB can be used on land and water. They are not a radio or telephone device, you cannot talk to anyone via them. You simply activate the unit when in a life threatening situation and, provided the unit has a clear view of the sky, it will detect passing satellites and send a distress message with your location to an emergency authority, who will then instigate a search and rescue for you. As

a result, don't activate the unit just to get help to change a tyre, otherwise you may find yourself responsible for the cost of issuing a search and rescue mission.

My advice is, if travelling in remote areas you should carry a PLB in case you find yourself in a life threatening situation. For more details and advice on these devices I suggest you consult www.gpsoz.com.au

global positioning system (gps)

The GPS has been around for quite a few years now. Primarily it locks onto satellites circling earth and by cross referencing with several satellites it determines your exact location. This information can be displayed on the GPS unit either via coordinates or via a visible map of the area in which you are located. A great help if you think you are lost. The GPS can do a lot more than just show your location, it also has the ability to store your route, list points of interest via their coordinates, determine travel time and arrival time based on current speed, display your compass bearing, ground speed and elevation.

Some GPS units are now combining city navigation

systems which replicate the traditional navigation systems that have become popular for motor vehicles. You can update your GPS with the latest map and street technology and even download your GPS information to a laptop which is tracking your progress on a detailed map of the area. For more details on these devices I suggest you consult www.gpsoz.com.au

spot

This is a brand name of a fantastic GPS device which I now use extensively in my four-wheel drive tour vehicles. This unit acts like a normal GPS, in that it identifies your coordinates. However, it does not display your location (at time of writing) on a screen but rather sends your location to an established website which uses Google maps and shows your exact position. This data is updated approximately every 10 minutes so it provides a very accurate picture of where you are at the time. This website can be given to family members and/or friends, they can log onto it and virtually follow you as you travel around Australia. Ideal for those who worry where you are, or for just keeping tabs on where you are going. I use it on my four-wheel drive tours to assist the families and friends of my customers to see where their loved ones are located at any given time. It also allows me to establish, at a glance, if my tour guide is on schedule or not. Check out my website www.4wd.net.au for my use of my SPOT device.

The SPOT device also provides a PLB function, and whilst its American branding indicates the emergency button as 911, if activated this will be the trigger point for the emergency rescue services to swing into action. For more details on the SPOT device I suggest you consult www.gpsoz.com.au

To wrap up communications, may I suggest that for the average outback traveller you should have a UHF radio for inter-car communication, a satellite telephone for emergency support and contact with family, and either a PLB or SPOT device for a real emergency situation (and with the SPOT, so family and friends can be forever envious of you and your travels). A combined street navigation and GPS unit might also be added.

outback bush camp

chapter 5

CAMPING GEAR

When selecting your camping gear for an outback trip it is important to remember the following; you are on holidays, you are supposed to be enjoying yourself and relaxing, therefore you should ensure you are comfortable. Over the many years that I've been travelling the outback I've seen all sorts of ideas on camping gear. Some are really good and others are just time and money wasters. So let's look at each item of camping gear and help you determine what is going to be right for you.

tents

On most outback trips it is safe to assume that you will be travelling quite a lot. This means that you will be making and breaking camp quite a bit. This immediately identifies that you should look for a tent that is easy and quick to erect and disassemble. There is nothing worse than fighting for half an hour with poles, ropes and canvas after a long day at the wheel. Whilst you are doing this your fellow travelling companions have erected their tent in only a few minutes and have already settled down to enjoy the sunset or relax around the camp fire.

A further consideration when choosing your tent comes under the heading of 'comfort factor'. Don't fall into the trap of choosing a small tent that packs away to a tiny bundle but gives you very little room once erected. No matter whether you are out for just two weeks or 12 months, unless you have a tent that gives you some space to move you will become quite frustrated.

Ideally your tent should allow enough room for you to stand up inside it. This makes getting dressed and attending to things, such as bathing more comfortable. This becomes even more important for the mature aged traveller who may not be as mobile as younger ones. Families also need plenty of space. Sharing a cramped, low slung tent with the kids for a few days whilst 'Hughie' is breaking the drought outside is not an enjoyable experience.

I have found the best type of tent that is quick to erect and gives plenty of useable space are the centre pole or 'bus' style tents. These tents are laid out on the ground, a tent peg inserted in each corner and then, using the centre pole, the roof and walls are lifted into place in one movement. The roof poles are permanently sewn into the tent and the centre pole lifts this up. You can have one of these tents fully erected in just a couple of minutes. More pegs can be added if required, especially if it's windy. With the centre pole in place the sewn in roof section should give you sufficient space to stand between the pole and the side of the tent without having to bend to avoid the canvas. Most good brands of this style of tent also offer an optional internal pole kit which replaces the centre pole, giving you even more space. Southern Cross Canvas, manufacture and supply excellent centre pole tents, and they're an Australian owned company, visit www.southerncrosscanvas.com.au

For two persons a three metre square tent is quite sufficient. A family can purchase the same style of tent but with an extended rear section, which does require another pole arrangement and takes about an extra two minutes to erect. These tents accommodate a family of four quite comfortably.

Another example of a fast to erect tent is the brand name OZTENT range of tents. Often touted as the 30 second tent, because it can be erected in virtually 30 seconds. The OZTENT comprises the length of the tent rolled up in a log style format. You simply lay it on the ground, fold out the floor section, then by holding the front opening of the tent you walk away from the rolled up tent, and as you do this the tent unfolds from itself and erects as the side poles are pulled forward and lock into place. Not only does

this tent erect quickly, it gives you plenty of space inside to stand and comes in a variety of sizes depending on the number of people you need to accommodate. The only downside to this style of tent is its overall length, with the smallest tent being 1.6metres long when packed away. It will not fit inside the average four-wheel drive, and therefore must be stored on the roof rack. You may not always need a roof rack, especially for a weekend trip, but the OZTENT basically requires one be carried. The OZTENT can also be quite heavy to lift up and down onto and from the roof rack and as you grow older this weight can become a chore.

When choosing your tent look for; a solid material on the floor, plenty of ventilation (at least a doorway and full window on opposite sides), and sewn in flyscreens. Always choose good quality canvas of either 10 or 12 ounce weight.

There are some excellent tents available in Australia, such as the Southern Cross Canvas and

OZTENT range, as well as some excellent overseas manufactured tents. However, no matter how good your tent is, never leave it packed damp. After just a few days, mildew will begin to destroy the canvas and stitching. Always make sure your tent is dry at the end of your trip, if it is packed wet then make sure you unpack it as soon as possible to dry, and certainly do not leave it folded up wet for any longer than two days .

Carry a ground sheet (the plastic type tarps are good but the shade cloth style material is better as it does not retain water) to place under your tent. This protects the floor of your tent from sharp sticks and burrs and helps to keep it clean. Secondly, place a doormat at the front door, you can purchase shower style mats from most camp stores. This is used to wipe the sand, mud or dust off your feet before entering the tent. In the desert regions the soles of your shoes will become encrusted with sharp burrs. It is a good idea to take your shoes off before entering the tent. Otherwise these burrs will get into your bedding and clothes and forever irritate you. Don't leave your shoes outside the tent overnight as dingos may steal them. Place your shoes in a plastic bag to keep the burrs and sand out of the tent, then bring the plastic bag in with you. Finally, carry a small brush and pan to sweep out your tent, you will be amazed how much dirt and sand gets in despite your best efforts.

In the Top End the weather can become very hot, even in winter. Expect midday temperatures in the high 30's and overnight around 20. Make sure your tent has plenty of ventilation. The ability to add an awning to your tent is also a good idea for those occasions when you do stop in the one place for a few days. This space can be used to accommodate the stove or just sit in the shade watching the world pass by.

Finally, always carry a few spare tent pegs and upgrade the pegs to large steel units of 25cm length. Add half a dozen sand pegs (large variety) for those sandy campsites in the deserts.

roof top tents

The roof top tent is mounted on your roof rack and generally occupies the whole of the roof rack. On reaching your campsite for the evening you simply park on level ground and commence the unfolding process. The tent is on a spring assisted system and quickly folds out to reveal the sleeping quarters. The bedding is usually left in place so you immediately have a place to rest. Some models form a covered area either beside the vehicle or to its rear, which can be used for meal preparation and shelter. A ladder provides access to the roof when its time to retire.

The advantages of this type of tent include its ease of erection, less effort in setting up the bedding compared to air beds, and the primary reason for choosing a roof top tent is that it gets you off the ground away from the creepy crawlies.

camping beside Cooper Creek at Innamincka, SA

However, in my opinion there are a few disadvantages to the roof top tent which I think need careful consideration. Obviously it takes up most, if not all, of the space on your roof rack so carrying extra spare tyres or firewood is out of the question. Secondly, if you have camped in a spot for more than one evening, but wish to take a short drive to a scenic site or into town to purchase supplies, the tent needs to be packed away. In addition, the roof top tent increases the centre gravity of your vehicle, even when you don't need to carry a roof rack on short outings, which in turn adds to the fuel use due to excessive wind drag across the roof. However, my greatest concern with the roof top tent is the ladder arrangement and accessing the tent, especially during the night when you have woken and have to visit the toilet. Climbing down from the roof on a small ladder in the dark and when half asleep, to me is a recipe for a disaster. Finally, the packing up process is quite strenuous with the need to access various corners of the tent to tuck them away, being on the roof this means access all around is required and will be difficult, especially for shorter, aged or less mobile persons.

swags

For outback travel the swag is a great idea. They are quick, convenient and very warm on those cold, winter nights. Their downside is that they offer you no privacy for getting dressed, are a little bulky when rolled up and offer limited protection from wet weather.

It is hard to beat the feeling of sleeping under the stars, and winter in the outback means clear skies. I use my swag extensively during my outback

journeys. But I still carry a small centre pole tent for when it is wet, or when I stay in the one spot for a few days and want protection from the flies, mosquitoes or wet weather. I always put a tarp under my swag for the same reasons that I described in the tent section. When choosing a swag look for one that offers; room between your head and the canvas, has a fully sewn in insect net, a window behind your head to allow ventilation, and for Top End travel where it is a lot warmer, the ability to throw back the canvas section and sleep under the insect screen without coming into contact with it. Always check the length and width of your swag before you buy it, some taller people will find the standard designs too short. Your swag manufacturer should be able to design a swag to suit your height and width.

air beds/mattresses

Choosing a good air bed or mattress is critical to enjoying your holiday. Getting a good night sleep is very important. After many years of camping and blowing up air beds with all manner of pumps I eventually found the self-inflating air mattress.

The problem with a conventional air bed is that it needs some means to inflate it, this usually means input by you using a manual pump, which can be a little hard on the back—or worse, the pump fails. Or you may have one of those fancy air pumps that run off your cigarette lighter. Again, it is something else to fail and all that racket sure scares the wildlife away. Once inflated the traditional air bed is not the most comfortable thing to sleep on. The air inside

the air bed chills very quickly on those cold desert nights and their design is not very supportive for your back. Finally, the old air bed always seems to spring a leak on the second night away.

The self-inflating air mattress totally does away with the need to carry a pump. You simply roll the mattress out, undo the nozzle and have cuppa or a coldie. Two or three puffs with your mouth after a few minutes to make the bed firm and you are set for the best night sleep. The mattress is filled with a foam rubber cell which sucks the air in. You sleep on this foam rubber which, once warmed by your body heat, stays nice and cosy all night. Even though the mattress is only a few millimetres thick you do not feel the ground through it. It is a firm bed once inflated, but this is why it is so good for your back. The mattress also prevents the transfer of moisture, so if your tent springs a leak on a wet, rainy night, your mattress will keep you dry.

There are various makes and sizes available these days in self-inflating air mattresses. The best advice is try before you buy, as the quality seems to vary with the price you pay—sometimes you do get what you pay for.

sleeping bags

Choosing the right sleeping bag is also very important. Remember that in the outback in winter, especially in the deserts, it will get very cold. Therefore, choose a sleeping bag that has a hood. You lose 85% of your body heat through your head, so to keep warm, keep your head covered. The other item to consider is the ability to turn over during your sleep. If the sleeping bag is too tight and restrictive you will not be able to move in your sleep, and this can lead to cramps, a stiff neck or back. I do not believe it is necessary to purchase a very expensive sleeping bag to get a good quality item. If you are into bushwalking and carry very little gear then a high tech sleeping bag costing hundreds of dollars is the only choice. But in your four-wheel drive there is plenty of room for a light but bulky item like a sleeping bag; with the added protection of a good tent or swag and a quality air mattress the thermal qualities of the expensive sleeping bag is wasted. As a rough rule choose a sleeping bag with a rating of minus five degrees Celsius, that costs around $150 to $200, with plenty of room and the ability to zip together to your partner's bag and you should not go wrong. Don't forget, when you travel into the northern regions the nights will warm up considerably and you will then want to be able use the bag as a cover rather than sleeping in it. The broad shaped bag fully zipped down one side and across the end easily unzips to become a doona cover for the warmer climates.

A good woollen blanket, like an army blanket, will help on those really cold nights; spread it over the air mattress under your sleeping bag. Don't be tempted to add extra blankets over the top of your sleeping bag, the duck down or similar material in the sleeping bag needs to loft (or fluff up) in order for it to provide maximum warmth efficiency. For this reason always unroll your sleeping bag as soon as you can allowing plenty of time for it to

loft before retiring. A full size pillow is a worthwhile addition; this can be used by passengers in the car as they doze away the miles and offers the right amount of support for your head at night.

car fridges

This has to be an essential item for anyone on a camping trip these days. There is a large variety of car fridges available and some work very well whilst others are not so efficient. Price is a good guide and I'm sorry to inform you that cheap is not always best. The well known brands such as Engel, ARB and Waeco are the standard to be considered. You need to choose a fridge that can keep its cool in the hottest conditions, one which can cool down to at least two degrees Celsius. Good fridges will handle this easily and can also be used as freezers. The two-way style fridge (240 watt and 12 volt), as manufactured by the brands mentioned, are the best choice. Avoid the three-way style fridge that offer gas operation as these fridges are notoriously less efficient and require level ground at all times for their most efficient operation, not always possible whilst travelling.

Don't be lured into purchasing a fridge that is too big. Before parting with your hard earned dollars make sure it fits into the rear storage space of the four-wheel drive without taking up all of the available space. Generally, a fridge in the 40-50 litre size will cater for your needs without consuming all of the available storage space. I have given some tips on how to carry food in your fridge in the *Food and Water Chapter*, see page 109.

The fridge is only as good as the wiring you run it off. Don't rely on standard equipment power outlets or cigarette lighters to power your fridge. For starters, these usually switch off when you turn off the ignition, and secondly they draw power from your main battery—the last thing you want to do is drain your starter battery. Also, in some cases, the wiring and fuses used in these accessory outlets don't maintain the current flow required to keep the fridge running and will either blow the fuse or even melt the wiring—possibly leading to a fire in the vehicle. The best bet is to have your four-wheel drive workshop install a power outlet in the rear of the vehicle wired directly to your second battery with its own fuse. Heavy duty wiring should be used and the plug designed so it cannot be easily dislodged by vehicle movement or other items packed around it.

Make sure your fridge is mounted on a spring base to help absorb the vibrations experienced off-road. I'm not a big fan of the expensive protection bags sold to cover your fridge as I have found these items actually scuff the fridge on corrugated roads—usually causing more damage than they are preventing. The fridge should be located in an area where its vents for heat dissipation and cooling are not totally covered, thus allowing the fridge to operate at maximum efficiency. Finally, keep a watchful eye on the operation of your fridge, if you notice that it is not maintaining its cooling you may be able to share your food with your travel companions (assuming you are travelling with others) rather than loose all your food. Alternatively use ice in the fridge pending repairs.

The downside to a good fridge is they are expensive, often in excess of $1000. This is hard to understand when that type of money can usually purchase a full size fridge for the kitchen at home. Some four-wheel drive accessory outlets have fridges for hire, so this may be another option, but don't skimp on the electrical fittings to run it as this is the most common cause for fridge failure.

If you decide to use your fridge as a freezer but still want to keep your drinks and margarine chilled, you might also carry an esky and some ice bricks. Carry at least four ice bricks in total, two in the freezer and two in the esky, alternating them each day. This keeps the esky chilled along with your drinks.

camp lights

In the old days everyone used the gas light and dolphin torch. Gas lights have been superseded these days. The idea of fitting a new mantle and carrying a spare glass for the gas light and the LPG to run it is a thing of the past. Gas lights are also a source of very high temperatures and can burn fingers or worse cause a fire if accidentally knocked over.

The modern four-wheel driver should carry a fluoro light. These lights run off your car battery, a ready available source of energy. They either plug into your cigarette lighter or clamp directly onto your battery terminals. Although, it is better to have your four-wheel drive workshop install extra power outlets for your camp lights which source their power from your second battery. This once again saves your main battery from being drained of its power.

The fluoro light produces a good white light with plenty of coverage; they make no noise in their operation and do not generate any heat. The fluoro light is very robust, rarely break and they can be used in your tent without fear of burning anything. Their portability means

they can be used to work under the vehicle or in the engine bay at evening if necessary.

When choosing your light look for a light that is reasonably compact, produces a strong white light, has a good length of lead (measure the distance from your vehicle to your tent, will it reach?) and does it have a switch on it so you can turn it off from the tent rather than having to unplug it from the car.

You will also need a torch or two, two is best. The Dolphin brand remains one of the best. Include at least one spare battery and one spare globe. There are many new lights available these days with LED lights becoming the latest trend. Small clamp on LED lights that fit to your hat or cap for working at night are a good idea and take up very little space. Camp stores even stock straps you can put around your forehead with a small battery powered light attached to it, ideal for setting up camp in the dark or cooking when you need both hands.

If travelling with children, make sure they have their own small torch, apart from ensuring that the batteries of the main camp torch are not run prematurely flat, they provide the children with a great source of entertainment. Kids love playing with torches after dark.

cooking stoves

There are many good cooking stoves on the market. When choosing your stove consider; the type of fuel it operates off, how easy it is to acquire this fuel and how easy it is to carry and use this fuel. For example, if you drive a diesel vehicle you may not wish to carry unleaded fuel for your stove. Carrying LPG gas is very safe and quite often someone else in your party may have a spare gas bottle if your bottle runs out.

Before you select your cooking stove think what you will be cooking on it. Determine the largest frying pan and saucepan you will want on the stove at the one time and take these items to the camping store. After choosing your stove check that your saucepan and frying pan actually fit over the burners together, quite often you may need to choose a three burner stove in order to get both of these items on the stove at the same time.

Also check for the wind protection on the stove and the adjustability of the heat. At a low heat setting is the wind protection sufficient? Always carry spare hoses and jets for your stove. Consider where you will set up your stove for cooking. Will you need a stand for it or will you put the stove on a table? Bending your back over the stove is not a good way to look after your self.

cooking equipment

When planning your menu determine what pots, pans and other items you will need to prepare your meals. Obviously do not take your best cooking utensils from the kitchen. Purchase camp quality cooking utensils from a respectable camping store. Choose items that can be used on an open fire or gas/fuel stove that won't be damaged by the heat— avoid plastic handles and Teflon style coatings. When packing these items away after use, pack

them so they won't rattle in the rear of the four-wheel drive. Use newspaper to separate the items, this also avoids unnecessary scratching and scoring of the utensils.

camp ovens

Nothing beats the taste of a camp oven cooked roast dinner—it can be the highlight of any camping trip. But there have been plenty of disasters in camp ovens also. The best advice is to select a camp oven of the appropriate size, one that will fit the roast or other meat selection that will feed the whole family. Whilst it is ideal to have a camp oven that can also accommodate your selection of vegetables, which allows the wonderful juices produced in the camp oven to marinate all the food, its not always possible to fit everything into one camp oven. Using a second camp oven for the vegetables may be a suitable alternative.

There are many good camp oven cookbooks available in camping stores that will give you all the tricks required for a successful camp oven dinner. My advice is to make camp early; have a ready supply of dry timber (the mulga in outback Australia is far more suitable than the hardwood timber of our mountainous areas); don't rush dinner by making the fire too hot; separate your cooking fire from your heating fire and practise as often as you can.

tables

When selecting a camping table it is best to avoid the type that has the seats attached. These can be either very heavy, or the light weight models simply fall apart during the trip. Having the seats attached to the table also means that you need to carry an extra set of camp chairs to sit around the camp fire after dinner.

The traditional style card table provides a good height at which to sit and enough room for two or

three people. They are a little bulky when folded up, so determine where you will pack it. Camping stores also have fold up camp tables of various sizes so again check for leg room and sturdiness of construction.

camp chairs

When choosing your camp chair try before you buy, take time to sit in it in the shop. Look for a chair that offers support to your back and shoulders and has some padding, this will keep you warm on those cold nights. Avoid the thin canvas types that have a bar across the front that cuts into the underside of your thigh. You might like a chair which has arms fitted for support, and finally determine the size of the chair when it is folded up and how well it will pack away. A chair that folds up into roughly a rectangular shape will always be easiest to pack,

Lochern National Park, Western Queensland

this style of camp chair provides head and shoulder support, which is very comfortable—you don't need to suffer when camping. Avoid a chair that has an open back section, this can provide a cold spot roughly where your kidneys are found, and this alone can lead to discomfort or soreness the next day. Some chairs fold up on themselves to form a neat round bundle, if these are comfortable for you then they may be a good choice. Like I said, sit in the chair for up to 30 minutes in the camp store before you part with any money.

portable showers and toilets

There really is no need to do without anything on your camping holiday. There is a wide range of portable showers available to the outback traveller; I have covered some of these in the *Preparing the Vehicle* chapter. However, an often overlooked item is the humble toilet. For many, especially the ladies and children, the thought of visiting the loo in the bush is enough to put them off camping. Remember, the more comfortable you can make the camping experience the more likely your partner is to want to embark on the adventure again and again. Many remote campsites are not served by any facilities, so it's a matter of finding a convenient bush. This is not always a desirable approach and in fact such bushes can be few and far between in some outback destinations.

When you arrive at camp select a location not too far away from your tent and erect one of those pop up shower tents, make sure you peg it down with some sand pegs, nothing will turn the family off

camping quicker than having the wind lift the toilet screen away from them at the most inconvenient time. Generally your camp will be on sandy ground (practically anywhere west of Dubbo has ground conditions like this) so it's relatively easy to dig a hole in the sand about 20 centimetres deep, leave the loose sand you have dug out of the hole in the enclosure with a small garden spade.

Camp stores have fold up toilet seats on legs, place this over the hole and you have your instant private latrine. The small hand spade and pile of loose sand is used by each visitor to cover their, for want of a better word, deposits. Thus avoiding the smell and flies for the next visitor. When breaking camp

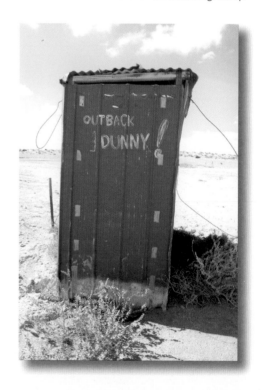

'bore bath', South-West Queensland

complete filling in the hole and pack away your personal toilet until next time.

For those times when you can't dig a decent sized hole or it's just a quick dash into the bushes whilst on the track it's still a great idea to teach everyone to bury their deposits. In fact, provided there is no risk of starting a raging bushfire I much prefer to suggest that you take a box of matches with you and burn your toilet tissue before burying it, this avoids the tissue being dug up by dingos and polluting the landscape.

Many caravans come equipped with their own onboard toilet system. However, this too needs to be emptied at some stage. Most caravan parks provide what they term as 'Dump points' to be used for this purpose. I have even seen Dump points provided in some country towns and along country roads, these are official Dump locations connected to the local sewage system or composting waste point. Unfortunately, I've also come across unofficial Dump locations, used by passing travellers where the person concerned has literally gone behind the nearest bush with their full tank from the caravan or chemical toilet and simply released the contents over the ground—not even bothering to bury the waste. It is unbelievable that anyone would pollute our pristine bush in this way when there are easily accessible Dump points in most towns or caravan parks. Please do the right thing and use these facilities.

It's easy to find where your nearest Dump point is located as there are several websites that will assist you. For example visit: www.sanidumps.com and click on the Australia link under the Country button, you could also visit the Campervan and Motorhome Club of Australia website at www.cmca.net.au Or even check out www.toiletmap.gov.au which lists all public toilets across Australia.

Canning Stock Route, Western Australia

chapter 6

FOOD & WATER

quarantine restrictions

There are several quarantine restrictions around Australia and it is best to become familiar with them rather than risk introducing a pest species to a healthy area or being fined for doing so. Contact Quarantine Domestic, tel: 1800 084 881 or visit www.quarantinedomestic.gov.au for state and quarantine borders and maps, details on all quarantine areas, along with what can and cannot be taken into these areas, and state contact information.

Further sites that may be of interest to the traveller include:

- South Australia, New South Wales and Victorian fruit growing areas – visit www.fruitfly.net.au
- New South Wales and Victorian Fruit Fly Exclusion Zone and Greater Sunraysia Pest Free Area – visit www.pestfreearea.com.au
- South Australian Fruit Fly Exclusion Zone – visit www.pir.sa.gov.au/planthealth/fruit_fly

water

containers

Don't carry all of your water in one container. There are two reasons for this. If the container springs a leak you will lose all your water at once and secondly, one 20 litre container is very heavy to lift whereas two 10 litre containers are much more manageable. It is important to consider how each person in your party will be able to cope with lifting heavy items, not everyone can easily manage a 20 litre water can.

Avoid plastic containers that split easily, these containers easily shatter on corrugated roads, and if accidently dropped, even a few centimetres. If you are not sure how sturdy your water container is before your trip, perhaps do the drop test, drop it when full from 15 centimetres and if it leaks, then

it's no good, better to find out at home than in the desert when water is scarce. Avoid containers that have screw in taps on their base, these rarely seal properly and will leak, also the tap is all too easily knocked when stowing the container, either snapping it off or causing it to leak.

I have found the best water containers are the 10 litre polypropylene (hard plastic style) containers you find in discount department stores, such as Kmart and Big W, or hardware stores. But always check them for leaks when you first purchase them—as sometimes the screw cap will not seal, no matter how hard you try to tighten it. Better to find out before you leave home than halfway up the Oodnadatta Track. Always store them standing up rather than lying down, if the cap should leak you won't lose all your drinking water and saturate the rear of the vehicle. Keep water containers behind the cargo barrier, as they make lethal missiles in a motor vehicle accident, and secure them to their resting place to avoid too much movement when travelling over rough ground or sand dunes. If you are concerned about them rubbing together or with other items in the rear of your vehicle, then place some marine carpet between each container or the other items they are stored with.

When you arrive in camp, remove one 10 litre container from its storage location and set it up in your camp for easy access by all those that may require it. This makes life easier for all users.

You may consider installing a water tank in or under your vehicle. Most four-wheel drive accessory outlets will have various styles of water containers for this purpose. I do have a couple of words of warning in this respect. Some bladder style water containers—those located on the floor under the feet of the rear passengers or in the cavities behind the cargo barrier—will over time, wear through where they naturally crease. Also, any water unit stored inside the vehicle should have a filler that is easily accessible. Not much point trying to take a gushing hose into the rear of your four-wheel drive. In addition, the outlets for these water containers need to be easily accessible, and positioned so that any leaks or spills will drain to the outside of the vehicle, rather than inside.

Polypropylene or stainless steel water tanks can be fitted in some cases under the vehicle. I have a unit like this in my Landcruiser. But be aware of where the filler is located and ensure that the filler neck allows a garden hose to be fully inserted in the filler pipe. The original filler hose on my water tank

had an aperture of less than 15mm and it was near impossible to fill. I changed it to a larger diameter and now I can insert a garden hose or even a funnel if filling from a water container.

The outlet for under vehicle water storage units can also be the source of great misery. Many are just small taps on the side of the tank under the vehicle, in my view a totally useless location for a water tap, as it is always covered in mud and other unsavoury items driven through on the track. Whilst it costs a few extra dollars, you won't regret installing a small in-line water pump that is plumbed to the rear of the vehicle and activated by a switch or tap switch at the rear of the vehicle. I have done this with my Landcruiser, and I have a ready source of water on tap to wash my hands. It really makes life very easy.

I suggest carrying all your water requirements initially from home, it is very easy for bore water or water from unknown sources to upset stomachs, and there can be nothing worse than an upset tummy on a camping trip. Of course, over time you will use this water and have to obtain water from these unknown sources. I always try to keep one container of home water for the purpose of taking pills or cleaning teeth. My other water is boiled in the billy, allowed to cool and then I decant it into my water containers. This will help keep the water tummy friendly. This water is generally used for cooking, washing and making a brew where it will either not be consumed or is boiled again. No matter how pristine the river system may look, always boil the water from it before drinking.

You can purchase water purifying tablets from camp stores but I suggest you try a variety of these before departing on your trip as some leave a very unpleasant taste in the water, it may be safe to drink but it tastes awful.

quantities

During your research for your trip you should ascertain where you can obtain reliable sources of water. This will help you determine how much total water you will need between these water points. A rough rule being 20 litres of drinking water will last a person five days in winter. In summer this should be increased to 40 litres per person for the same period. As an example, in winter I recommend 20 litres of water per person when travelling across the Simpson Desert, but after September this is increased to 40 litres per person. This may seem like a lot of water but I am being realistic, and recognise that a lot of drinking water actually gets used for washing, cleaning teeth etc.

food

plan a menu

If your travels in the outback will be for only a few weeks it is a good idea to plan a menu before you head out. This will help you determine what you will need to carry and ensure that you do not carry a lot of food that is wasted. There is no reason why you can not eat just as good whilst camping as you do at home. Provided you have the appropriate sauces, stock cubes, and all those other condiments that

Gecko

make a great meal you should be able to replicate your culinary skills whilst camped in the outback.

However, before you race out and start buying all the goodies it might be a good idea to check what quarantine areas you will be travelling through. See *Quarantine Restrictions* at the start of this chapter on page 109. With your menu planned for week one, you can either simply repeat it for week two and three and so; or you might be really inventive and be able to plan a menu for each week you are away. Naturally you will need to resupply at some time during your trip, but your pretrip research will tell you where this is best done. Don't forget to take advantage of the culinary delights for which some of our famed destinations are known. For example, whilst you cannot take fresh fruit into Western Australia, if you are travelling through the Kimberley Region you can find no better place for fruit than the town of Kununurra on the edge of the Ord River Irrigation Scheme.

meat

The best way to carry meat is to have it vacuum sealed or cryovacced. This is a process where the meat is wrapped in plastic and the air is extracted from the package. It means the meat will last for several days without the need for freezing. It must still be refrigerated, but this is much easier than trying to keep it frozen when the other items in your fridge only need to be chilled.

Quite a number of butchers provide the vacuum sealing service even in country towns, so just ask around until you find one that does. Some may charge a little extra whilst others don't.

Vacuum sealed red meat will keep in the fridge at around two degrees for up to six weeks. It is best

to make sure that any bones are removed as these can rub through the plastic packing destroying the vacuum seal. White meat will only last for about seven days and be careful with sausages and rissoles that contain a lot of onion and other seasoning as these will only last a few days. If the sealed bag begins to blow up, it is best not to eat the meat.

fruit and vegetables

Carrying these items is essential in order to have a good, healthy meal each day. But due to the crushing that can occur in the back of the four-wheel drive, and the pounding they receive on rough roads, as well as the heat that builds up in your vehicle, they can spoil very easily. When determining your menu the soft skinned items like tomatoes and bananas will need to be consumed within three days of purchase, they rarely last much longer than this no matter how well you pack them. Make sure that items like lettuces do not freeze in the fridge overnight, as this will ruin them.

The best advice I can give you is wrap all your fruit and vegetables separately in newspaper. This creates a buffer for the items and stops the scuffing and squashing. Also, if one item does go off it doesn't ruin the other items packed with it. Check your food at least every second day, because the sooner you find a problem the less damage will be done. The used newspaper can be stored for wrapping more items next time you replenish the larder, and as the contents of the food box gets lower can be used as packing.

glass

If carrying items that come in glass containers you should wrap the glass in bubble wrap. This is available from post offices and stationery suppliers. This will prevent the glass from breaking on the rough roads. It is even better if you are able to remove the contents from the glass bottle and carry it in a sealed plastic container. Always choose square shaped containers as these are easier and more efficient to pack.

Remember, when the glass container is empty you must carry it out with you—it will still need to be wrapped in the bubble wrap to prevent breakage. Never throw old bottles in the camp fire as they will shatter and then you must carry the broken glass with you until you can dispose of it correctly. Never bury broken glass—dingos always dig up whatever you bury.

cans

Canned food can become very bulky and heavy so try to keep this to a minimum. Be careful with any cans that have ring-pull tops as these can easily have their seal broken by other cans bouncing on them over rough roads. When packing them you might consider placing layers of bubble wrap between any cans that are stacked on top of each other. Aluminium cans are often a problem as they tend to rub through on the corrugated roads. It may be best to wrap each can individually in either newspaper or bubble wrap. Be careful when carrying your beer too, as the aluminium cans frequently rub through in their cartons. You should check your canned food and drinks for wear marks at regular intervals as you may be able to prevent further damage occurring once you become aware of it.

drinks

Milk at the start of any trip can be carried in the plastic two litre containers but be careful that you do not drop it into the fridge as they have a tendency to fracture and leak if treated in this way. When the plastic container is empty do not throw it away, it can be used to hold your UHT or powdered milk. UHT milk does not have to be refrigerated until it is opened and then it will need to be transferred out of its waxed or plastic coated cardboard container. However, be careful with these containers as they become quite weak around the bottom edge whilst being transported in your food box. The vibrations caused by corrugated roads weaken the bottom edge of the

container. This weakness results in weeping and leakage which then ruins all the other items stored in your tucker box.

The same can be said for any juices, custards or creams that are supplied in these types of waxed or plastic coated cardboard containers. It is a good idea to wrap these items in a sealed plastic bag which will retain any spillage that occurs, or pack them into a plastic container of their own which again ensures that if they weep it doesn't contaminate everything else. You should also turn these containers upside down each day, this reduces the risk of the container weeping by prolonging the strength of the bottom edge of the container.

Plastic one litre bottles of soft drink are better than carrying cans, as they do not rub through as easily and when the bottle is empty it can be used to transfer liquids from other packages that do not travel so well. Be careful with hard, brittle plastic fruit drink bottles, if you accidentally drop them they will fracture and leak. Even a short drop of a few millimetres into the esky or fridge will cause the plastic bottle to break, so make sure that the kids treat them carefully when helping themselves to a drink.

storage containers

The storage of your food and other utensils is most important. Once a can is open the contents need to be stored safely and securely. I recommend that you carry an assortment of square or rectangular shaped Decor or Tupperware style containers for this

purpose. Make sure the lid seals correctly; there is nothing worse than the contents of your container spreading itself throughout your fridge. The square and rectangular containers are much easier to pack in your food boxes or fridge and make the best use of space, avoid round containers wherever possible.

For milk and other liquids like cooking oil; strong, resealable drink containers, the square type, make the best use of space and pack more solidly. If carrying butter or margarine, you should take the butter/margarine out of its shop container and transfer it to a container whose lid you know will not come off. You need to realise that on tracks in our desert country there will be many times when the rear of your vehicle jumps up and down, this causes the contents of everything packed in the back and everything packed in the fridge to jump up

and down. Any loose lids will simply fly off and the contents of the container will spread throughout your fridge or food box.

Saucepans and frying pans rarely come in square shapes but these can be packed in a square crate (the milk crate style) and then be padded with newspaper or similar to stop them rattling and rubbing together.

some general hints on food storage and meal preparation

Carry a roll of paper towels which can be used in various ways around the camp kitchen such as wiping out pans, plates and utensils before washing up; cleaning up spills and wiping hands whilst cooking instead of rinsing, when water is scarce.

Mulga country, outback New South Wales

Also, keep a roll of aluminium foil in your kit as this is great for marinating red meat, cooking fish so the seafood oil doesn't permeate your barbecue plate or fry pan, and for wrapping potatoes to cook straight in the hot coals. Not much else beats a potato cooked in the hot coals, smothered in butter, with a dash of salt. Just scoop the cooked potato out of its skin with a small spoon—absolutely delicious, or better still, top it with some sour cream!

Carry a container of wet-ones, try to get them in an oblong plastic box as it packs better. These are used for keeping your hands clean when preparing meals or in the vehicle when travelling to refresh the face and hands.

Bread is readily available in most towns, even those that don't have large supermarkets or bakeries. You will usually find frozen bread in the freezer in the service station or general store. However, if travelling in the peak season (winter and school holidays), remember that these locations have a great demand on their supplies. The towns that carry frozen bread don't have their own bakery so it is brought in by truck once a week and therefore, in the busy tourist times, they can run out of supplies.

Try making your own bread or damper in the camp oven if you know supplies are going to be short. It is best to practise some of the bread recipes from your specialist camp oven cookbook before you depart on your big trip as there is a skill to correctly cooking bread in a camp oven.

Dried foodstuffs can be handy. For example noodle meals make good stand-bys when you want something quick and easy. Give yourself at least one night off a week with these stand-by types of meals. Get the square-shaped packets rather than the foam cup or polystyrene rounded bowl-types as they pack better. You can make some of these noodle dishes quite tasty with your own ingredients— chicken noodles become quite delicious and creamy with a raw egg stirred through them. A tin of creamed corn is another additive that gives the noodles body. Left over roast meat, ham or bacon chopped into beef noodles is also worth trying. Chinese flavoured noodles go well with prawns (can be tinned), asparagus and cheese, tinned tomatoes, or diced vegetables.

Alex, the damper king

waterhole on the Hardey River - Pilbara region, Western Australia

chapter 7

PERSONAL NEEDS

clothing

The main issue here is—don't take too many clothes. If you are setting out for your annual holidays and have decided to drive across the Simpson Desert or up Cape York consider that you will be surrounded by dust all the time. You will never stay immaculately clean—so why try? I'm not suggesting that you go completely feral, but accept the fact that you will get dirty, and it is impossible to have a clean outfit every day. Space and weight in your four-wheel drive will be at a premium, anything you can do to reduce it will be welcome. There are certain things, like fuel and water, which you must take but it is not essential to have a fresh set of clothes each day.

The type and amount of clothing you require will vary depending on where and when you travel. A Simpson Desert trip in winter will require plenty of warm clothes including a jumper and wind jacket, as well as long pants. Travel in this same area later than October, and you will live in T-shirts and shorts. The Top End, above the Tropic of Capricorn in winter, is very mild during the day, with temperatures ranging from the mid 20's to the high 30's. But, anywhere more than 50 kilometres from the coast, night temperatures can still drop to single figures, so make sure you have a jumper and some track pants for the nights around the camp fire.

Whilst travelling take two or three changes of comfortable clothes suited to the region you are visiting. These shirts, jeans etc can be worn for two to three days. Yes, they will get dirty from the dust on the vehicle and from the usual camp fire

activities, but out there, who cares! It is a good idea to have a pair of old overalls to change into if you have to work on the vehicle or climb under it to check on anything. This saves you from getting really dirty in one go, and stops the burrs that stick to your clothes from spreading throughout the vehicle and your clothes bag. Keep the work overalls in a separate garbage bag for this reason.

It is also a good idea to carry a set of neat casual clothes that you can use when you reach a town and decide to have dinner at the local club or restaurant.

A hat with a broad brim will be needed for sun protection; this is particularly important in the Top End, from Cape York across the Gulf through Darwin and over the Kimberley region to Broome, where even in winter the sun will burn you. A pair of

sunglasses is also worth having. In Central Australia during winter a beanie for those cold nights around the fire is a must, you lose 85% of your body heat through your head, so keep it covered!

You will most likely do quite a lot of walking on your outback trip. Therefore, a good pair of walking boots will be essential. When choosing your walking boots it is best to consider the terrain in which they will be used. Most of the outback consists of sandy ground covered in sharp spinifex needles and assorted grass seeds that just love to get into your socks. In some parts of the Kimberley and Pilbara you can expect some very rough rocky areas with razor sharp stones that can make short work of runners, and really make a mess of unprotected feet in sandals. This is why I recommend elastic sided boots rather than lace up boots. The laces will become a mass of burrs in no time. In the warmer climates you will most likely be wearing shorts and as a result your socks will be exposed to the spinifex and burrs, for this reason you should take a pair of over socks or sock savers. You will find these in any good camping store or work clothing outlet.

Always carry a pair of bathers or swimming costume, as even in winter the joys of a dip in Dalhousie Springs in the Simpson Desert is one of the wonders of the outback world. Whilst in the north there are many rivers that are crocodile safe which cannot be passed without a swim. One towel per person is plenty, as these weigh quite a lot. This towel can be used for normal showering as well as your 'beach towel' when enjoying a remote river. In the north it will dry very quickly whilst in winter in Central

Australia, just lay your wet towels over your luggage behind the cargo barrier and they will dry during the course of the day's travel.

If travelling between October and April in Central Australia, and at most other times in warmer climates, you can expect to share your holiday with thousands of bush flies. These little critters can drive you to absolute distraction and may even ruin your holiday. Purchasing a fly net that stretches over your hat and under your chin would be a great investment. Insect repellent can be carried but has little effect on the millions of bush flies. If you are destined to travel in the warmer months it would be wise to invest in one of those insect screen style marquees with fully netted walls. This will prove to be a safe haven for you when it comes time to cook and eat a meal. Without it you will struggle to have a peaceful meal without sharing it with hundreds of bush flies, not a pleasant experience at all.

swimming in Dalhousie Springs, Simpson Desert

washing clothes

Never wash your clothes, or yourself, in rivers or in stock watering holes, this pollutes the streams and stock water. Transport the water away from its source and wash your clothes in a tub which can double as a container used to carry food or the cooking utensils (a square container is recommended). Make sure that you pack: a length of clothes line and enough pegs to take care of your needs; some washing powder, in a container that doesn't split open or leak; and maybe a small plastic scrubbing brush for those stubborn stains. When you do reach a town and stay in a caravan park there will be a rush for the washing machines, make sure you get up early and have plenty of dollar coins at the ready.

Many camp stores sell washing buckets with a sealable lid. The idea is to place your clothes in the bucket with some water and washing powder, seal the lid and strap the bucket to the roof rack. During the day's travel the water agitates like a washing machine and cleans your clothes. It works well, but that big round bucket takes up heaps of storage space and, by now, you will have learnt that I like square or rectangular containers to make best use of space in the vehicle.

health

Staying healthy on your holidays is of paramount importance. Apart from not wishing to spoil your long awaited holiday, who wants to be sick in the outback, when they are away from the comforts of home?

Before you leave on your journey have a talk with your doctor. Make sure that you have enough quantities of any medicines that you need to get you through your trip. Remember that not all outback towns will have a pharmacy that can renew a prescription. Larger regional towns such as Broken Hill, Port Augusta, Alice Springs and Kununurra will have a pharmacy or chemist, but there are none in-between. So plan how long you will be travelling between these points and make sure that you have all the personal needs that you require.

Get your doctor to give you a prescription for vomiting and diarrhoea tablets. These are the best way to combat this unpleasant occurrence if you are away from facilities. Also ask your doctor to prescribe the necessary medication to counter infection from dirty wounds, as keeping clean in the outback can be tricky. An infected cut on your hand can quickly become very serious and is not to be ignored. Your research before leaving home should identify where medical help is located in the isolated regions and the contact number for the local Royal Flying Doctor Service.

Carry a supply of headache pills as well as band aids. Naturally you should have a comprehensive first-aid kit in the four-wheel drive and both partners should be first aid trained. Contact St John's Ambulance or the Red Cross for training course details and available first-aid kits.

When bush camping normal hygiene often gets ignored as the availability of water is not quite as easy at it is at home. But don't compromise your

health. Always wash hands after attending to toilet needs and wash before handling food.

When you stop in a caravan park or camping area that has communal shower facilities it is wise to always wear a form of foot covering such as a pair of thongs when showering. There are still a lot of bugs lurking on the floors of shower cubicles and some campgrounds in remote areas certainly do not receive the cleaning that we expect. For this reason, it is also a good idea to carry some treatment, powder or cream, for tinea infections of the feet. It is very easy to pick-up something like this from communal showers, so after each shower apply the treatment to your feet and you should be OK.

Something else, you may not be aware of, that will happen to everyone that travels in the outback is the effect of the dry air on our skin. Living on the coast where the air is moist it is easy to forget how much drier the air is in Central Australia, even in winter. After only a few days in the outback with the constant wind and dry air, that is common in

winter months, you will find that your lips and hands will dry and begin to crack. This will happen to both men and women. It might be seen as macho to tough it out, but this is only inviting trouble. Remember, that in your travels the normal levels of hygiene and availability of water is greatly reduced. As a result, the chances of infection are increased. To combat the effects of the dry air carry lip cream, applying it throughout the day and at night, and some moisturising hand cream. Yes, even the men should use this, as the skin around the finger nails will dry and split creating nasty sores.

Travelling in the winter in the desert country it is very cold at night and there is always a constant wind. Sitting around a blazing hot fire at night is common but this combination of chill air and fierce heat from the fire is very conducive to chill blains, especially on the ears, which are exposed to the cold air. Even if you do not normally suffer from this ailment you may find that this can become a problem on your holiday. Carry some cream to combat this problem and to relieve the burning itch that usually develops. To avoid it in the first place, keep your ears covered by your beanie at night at all times and you will avoid the painful burning ailment.

If a member of your party uses ventolin, it would be a good idea to carry a couple of spares.

Finally, to avoid nasty bites from mosquitoes and sandflies, it is suggested that you take vitamin B tablets for at least one week prior to departing on your trip, and then throughout your travels. This does not actually stop them biting you, but eases

Alice Springs, 'Capital' of the Red Centre

cards or they are stolen this will help when making the necessary phone calls as soon as possible. It might also be a good idea to establish which towns have a branch of your own bank to assist in accessing further quantities of cash from your account if needed.

Always keep an emergency quantity of money at hand in case of major breakdown, illness or other unforseen occurrence.

the itch that follows. If you are going into an area infested with sandflies you should apply a mix of baby oil (eight parts) and Dettol (one part) liberally to your exposed skin. This should stop sandflies from having you for lunch, as well as soothe any previous bites. Sandfly bites should not be taken too lightly, they have been known to become infected and create a serious health risk, at the least, the little itchy bites will make your life a misery for several days.

money

You will always need to carry some cash with you, the more remote the location the less likely it is that they will accept credit cards. Also, American Express cards are frowned upon in many locations so if you are carrying plastic then make sure you have an alternative to Amex. Keep contact numbers for your credit cards in a safe place; if you lose your credit

Buley Rockhole, Litchfield National Park, Northern Territory

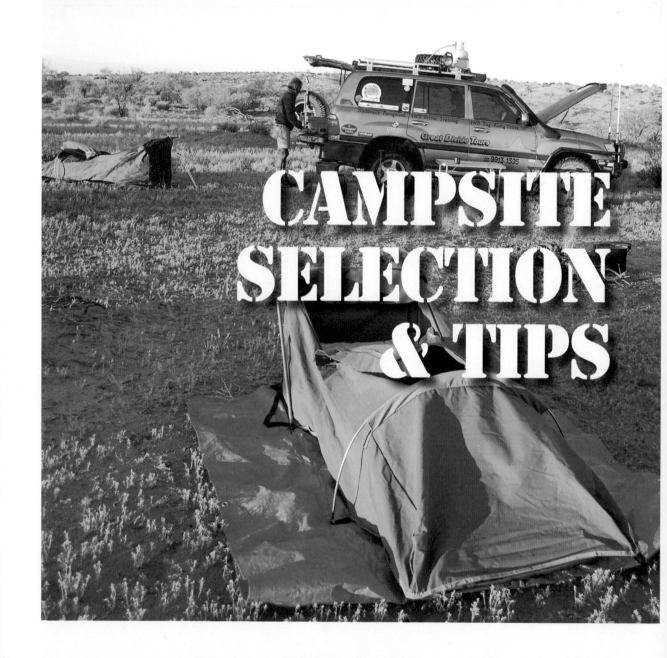

chapter 8

CAMPSITE SELECTION & TIPS

I recall on one of my four-wheel drive tag-along tours, as we travelled up the west side of the Simpson Desert, I found an amazing campsite amongst some trees beside the only billabong for a hundred kilometres, it was an ideal setting amidst a barren landscape of rocky plains. There was quite a deal of discussion amongst my travelling companions how I could seemingly pull a fabulous campsite literally out of thin air. There was even vigorous discussion that despite my statement that I had not travelled this way previously, that I must have known that this one perfect location existed. The truth of the matter was I had not been to this location before but I just kept looking for the right signs to indicate what might be a good campsite, on that day I got lucky. But, as anyone who has travelled with me will attest, I seem to get lucky, most of the time, when looking for a campsite. This makes me think, there must be a knack to it, so here are some of my secrets to finding a perfect campsite.

how to choose a great campsite

So here you are on your great outback adventure trundling through the endless red centre, the day has worn on and it's getting close to time to make camp. Assuming you are not actually aiming for a known location such as Dalhousie Springs, Durba Springs or Butterfly Springs, but you are on a seemingly endless red plain with scattered spinifex and the occasional red sand dune, how do you find that perfect campsite? There are several clues that I look for, here they are in no particular order.

- Don't leave it until right on sunset to start looking for a camp, especially if you are in country that doesn't look too inviting.
- Start your observations from no later than 4pm and, even possibly 3.30pm in winter when there is little light left by 5pm.
- If you stumble across a fantastic spot earlier and your itinerary permits, then don't pass it up, make an early camp. I stopped for lunch once beside the flooded Eyre Creek in the Simpson Desert and after munching my SAO's declared to our group that we were camping the night here, most people didn't believe me, but it turned out to be one of the best camps I've ever had.
- Don't expect to find the perfect spot first time every time, also be prepared to double back if the following sites are not as good as the first.

- If I see wheel tracks heading off the track or road it's always worth exploring them, sometimes they just lead to a barren stockyard but other times they have led to the most idyllic campsite, there was one like this on the Gary Junction Road near Pollock Hills.

- If in sand dune country (for example up the Birdsville Track) wait until the sand dune beside the track which you have been paralleling for some time crosses the track. This allows you to drive up the swale between the sand dune ridges away from the track and you will always find a great level campsite between the dunes within 500 metres of the track. Far enough away from the road to avoid prying eyes and usually with an abundance of mulga firewood surrounded by rich red dunes, idyllic!

- In the above scenario, don't leave the road and drive over the sand dunes as your wheel tracks will leave their mark   for years to come, and others will only follow.

- In the dry barren country where the ground is littered with gibbers (small stones) and little else, the prospect of finding a good camp may seem very slim. You may

camping along the Birdsville Track

have to travel for some distance just to see the slightest undulation, but eventually you will spot a row of shrubs and possibly even trees snaking their way across the landscape. These shrubs will provide a wind break from the constant breeze in the outback and even a source of firewood in a landscape that resembles the moon surface (never cut trees or bushes down for firewood, only use what has already fallen and then sparingly as even the dead timber provides home for the desert animals).

- Don't be tempted to camp in dry creek beds as flash floods may occur without warning, even though it may not be raining where you are located. Use these dry river beds to access areas that make great camps. Where the track crosses the dry river, either follow the river bed (the soft sand may require you to drop tyre pressure) or follow the high side of the bank. I usually find an ideal level spot even with a bit of shade out of the river bed within 500 metres of the track.

- A word of warning, when looking for your camp and you are driving off the road, be very careful of your wheel placement. The hard mulga stumps can easily pierce the sidewall of your tyres. I've even had very small, hard as rock, twigs stab right through the tread of the tyre. So

Camping in the West MacDonnell Ranges, Northern Territory

keep a keen eye on where you are driving as you explore the terrain.

- In the early stages of the Canning Stock Route much of the ground is rocky and very hard, I resorted to carrying a tent peg and hammer with me. Every time I left the track to look for a level campsite, I tested the ground with the tent peg, if it wouldn't penetrate the hard surface I moved on.

- When selecting your campsite look for ants' nests on the ground and lots of cobwebs hanging from trees, if you see these, move on. You don't really want to share the night with either of these desert dwellers.

- Don't camp beside stock watering holes or obvious wildlife water spots, if necessary move a hundred metres away from billabongs, this will still allow the wildlife to quench its first at the end of the day, and provide a magic nature vista for you.

- There are some fantastic beach camping opportunities around our vast coast, but actually camping on the beach means you will be forever contending with a sharp, cool breeze. Instead, follow the swales between the sand dunes behind the beach, avoid driving on any vegetation, and you will often find a level spot large enough to camp. The surrounding sand dunes protect you from the ever present wind and you will have your camp to yourself.

- In spinifex country it's not always easy to find a clear piece of ground. In this situation carry a spade or shovel with you and use it to clear a

small patch of ground large enough for your tent and camp fire. Don't ever burn off the spinifex to clear an area as the fire will get away from you and might burn for days or weeks. I've visited spots 12 months after I had cleared it using a spade and found them to have totally regrown, so the impact of this style of camping is very minimal.

- Seeking permission to camp on someone's property is the correct thing to do. Much of the outback is located on private land or aboriginal land. However, it is not always possible to seek permission as finding the station homestead on a million hectare property is like finding a needle in a haystack. Therefore, always respect the land you are camped on. Don't cut fences; leave gates as you find them; never leave any rubbish behind; bury all human waste and burn off toilet paper if safe to do so; keep clear of stock watering holes and never harass livestock.

- Never leave your camp fire burning or smouldering when you leave camp. However, you need to be very careful if you decide to extinguish your fire before leaving camp using just water. The pouring of water into your camp fire might seem like the right thing to do but if done recklessly, it can lead to severe injury. Never, poor water directly into a pit of hot coals, this can cause a minor explosion as the water hits the coals and literally blow the hot coals up and over you or at least fill your eyes with ash from the fire. Your fellow campers won't take too kindly to their camping gear or vehicle being showered in the ash that this action will generate either. The best method of ensuring your outback fire is safe to leave is to bury it with sand and then poor water over the sand allowing it to seep slowly down onto the hot coals.

camp fire tips

When you select your campsite in a remote area dig a fire pit about 20 centimetres deep and 40 centimetres wide. If you carry a piece of steel mesh or reo you can place this over one end of your fire pit. With a good bed of hot coals under the mesh it makes cooking on the open fire very easy. Just place your billy, pots and other cooking vessels on the mesh, and add small amounts of timber to the fire as required to maintain the heat. The other end of the fire can be built up to provide heating for those sitting around the fire and as a ready source of hot coals for camp ovens. The timber in the outback burns very easily and provides a great bed of hot

coals in no time at all. You do not need a lot of wood to maintain a good cooking fire.

Firewood can be scarce at popular campsites, so to save further denuding the vegetation in the popular areas, it is suggested that you collect your firewood requirements about 30 minutes before stopping and making camp. Always wear leather gloves when collecting your firewood to avoid nasty scratches and splinters which can easily become infected, hygiene and cleanliness whilst camping is not at its best.

When you leave camp use the sand or soil that you removed from the fire pit to cover the coals in the fire. The mulga coals can stay red hot for several days and a strong gust of wind can flick a burning ember out of the fire pit into nearby spinifex causing a wildfire. By burying your coals you avoid this possibility and the area you leave behind is virtually untouched except for a few foot prints which will quickly disappear in the dry shifting sands of the desert. As detailed previously pour some water over

Cooper Creek near Windorah, South-West Queensland

easily suffer a severe cut even when trying to do the right thing and carrying it out with you. Avoid glass containers wherever possible, but if not possible keep the empties in a safe and separate container until you reach an appropriate refuse disposal area.

camping etiquette

When you select a campsite and others are in the area don't camp right on top of them—move to the furthest point away to make your camp. Keep noise to a minimum and be respectful of others needs. Don't drive through camping grounds at a speed that raises enormous quantities of dust, respect other people and their quiet enjoyment of the surrounds. Don't play loud music or radio broadcasts when in camp, listen to the symphony of the bush. If I had my way I would ban generators, but if you must use one, locate it well away from other campers and turn it off by 9pm

the sand, it will seep through the sand and extinguish the hot coals.

Never leave any rubbish at your campsite—the old days of burn, bash and bury are long gone. By all means burn your rubbish at the end of the evening to reduce the quantity and dispose of food waste, but remove any tins, silver foil or unburnt material before you leave your camp. Remove all evidence of your rubbish by carrying either a strong plastic garbage bag or one of those rubbish packs that attach to your spare tyre on the rear door.

Never dispose of glass products in the bush or in the camp fire, the glass will break in the camp fire and then be a hazard to any following campers. Broken glass is also very dangerous to carry and you can

if not earlier. If you are an early riser, don't expect everyone else in the camp to be also, keep your noise to a minimum.

If you are travelling with children teach them to respect other people's privacy and belongings. Children should not be permitted to play ball games or throw objects close to other campers; there is plenty of space in Australia without allowing your children to play on top of other people. Don't allow children to run around camp fires, this is a recipe for a serious accident and in the bush you are a long way from help. If children insist on cooking marshmallows over the open fire supervise them, otherwise someone is going to get burnt or poked in the eye with a burning stick. Don't allow children to place timber on the fire, they will just end up burning themselves.

chapter 9

OUTBACK DRIVING TIPS

driving on unsealed roads

Most of your driving in your four-wheel drive is likely to be on well-formed gravel roads. A trip around Australia visiting some of our better-known four-wheel drive destinations will involve 90% of good to reasonable gravel or formed earth roads. Actual four-wheel drive is not required for this type of road but the attributes of the four-wheel drive (such as large wheels, heavy duty suspension and strong chassis construction) are best suited to this type of driving. The tracks that conjure up visions of the true outback and those that are the foundation of our great escape dream—such as the Birdsville Track, the Oodnadatta Track, the Strzelecki Track, the Gibb River Road, the Tanami Track and even most of Cape York—comprise good gravel or earth formed roads.

You can safely travel at speeds up to 100 km/h on these roads. But your driving style needs to be correct to avoid potential disaster. These roads all have the same common trait. They are graded in a gentle curve with a distinct crown on the road. This is done to allow water to quickly drain off the surface when and if it does rain. This type of road construction requires some unique driving skills and presents road hazards to the unwary or inexperienced driver.

The crowning of gravel roads result in drivers travelling on the very top or centre of the road. This is the smoother path and keeps the vehicle away from the shoulder of the road. Because drivers in both directions occupy the centre of the road, any loose stones on the surface are pushed to each side. The result is a relatively smooth section of road down the centre of the track and lots of loose stones on the shoulder. The smooth section of gravel provides good tyre grip and allows reasonably high speeds to be maintained. However, if the driver strays to either side of the road where the loose

stones have been pushed the available traction is greatly reduced. It is very easy for a four-wheel drive, or any vehicle for that matter, to lose traction in these circumstances and slide out of control off the road. If towing a camper trailer or caravan this straying to the edge of the road can lead to severe swaying of the camper trailer or caravan and end in a roll over.

unsealed roads and corners

As the road follows a corner, the 'line' most commonly used becomes clear of loose stones, which pile up on the outside edge of the corner. Provided the driver keeps out of these loose stones, good traction can be maintained, even without the use of four-wheel drive. However, if the driver finds that he or she needs to move to the outside edge due to an oncoming vehicle or deep rut or pothole on the apex of the corner, look out! Once the vehicle hits the loose stones piled up on the shoulder of the corner, the four-wheel drive will lose traction and

can easily slide out of control. The correct approach to any corner on good outback roads is to slow down to a speed that will not result in the vehicle losing control if it moves off the 'line' and into those loose stones.

When approaching a corner on a gravel road, maintain the vehicle on the hard-packed surface, keep out of the loose stones on the edge of the road and slow down, using the brakes gently. Then gently accelerate through the corner. If an oncoming vehicle is observed in advance, slow down well before the corner and move gradually into the loose stones on the shoulder. Go as slowly as is necessary, as any excess speed whilst turning on loose stones will result in a slide and possible excursion off the track. Avoid sharp steering inputs as these too will result in a slide from the front wheels and no steering response. Similarly, do not brake heavily as the tyres will easily lock up where there are loose stones. ABS (Anti Brake Skid—an anti-locking brake device) will activate in these circumstances and your vehicle, instead of slowing down for the corner, may maintain the speed at which it was travelling, which can be very disconcerting.

Also be aware that in areas where there are trees or bushes growing up to the edge of the road, you will not be able to see well ahead and you can quickly come across an approaching vehicle. This reduces your reaction time and usually results in you swerving and braking too sharply as you enter the loose stones, a sure recipe for disaster. In these conditions the best advice is; drive at a speed that allows you plenty of time to safely negotiate the

Track to The Lost City, Litchfield National Park, Northern Territory

corner, even if you have to move to the edge to allow an oncoming vehicle to pass.

If you are midway through a bend and a large pothole or rut appears on the apex of the bend, avoid the urge to slam on the brakes or swerve violently to avoid it. This can easily result in the four-wheel drive sliding off the track and possibly overturning as it hits the bank or culvert. Instead you should brake gently and make minor steering adjustments to avoid the worst of the pothole or rut. But again, the best advice is to slow down and take your time with every corner. You should drive defensively as it could save you from a major accident and ruining your holiday.

controlling a slide

The correct method for controlling a slide on an unsealed road is to turn the steering into the direction of the slide, but not too much. Initially you should lift off the accelerator to decrease the speed and avoid using the brakes. Once you have regained some control of the vehicle then gently accelerate to drive the vehicle back onto the intended and safe line.

If the vehicle fishtails or slides out in the opposite direction to the first slide, correct the steering into the opposite direction, always steering into the slide. Gently apply the brakes as you do so. Do not let go of the steering wheel, keep a firm hold throughout the process. After you have regained control of the vehicle it is good idea to pull over and stop. Check your tyres for any damage; especially look around

the rim of the wheel where stones and grit may have been forced between the tyre and the rim. Replace the tyre if it shows any sign of damage or forced intrusion by grit and stones between the tyre and rim, and have it checked by a qualified tyre-fitter or repairer as soon as possible. Also, check the pressure in each tyre, the slide and loss of control may have been caused by a slowly deflating tyre in the first place.

corrugations

The scourge of outback travel is corrugations on unsealed roads. Whether you are driving up the Oodnadatta Track, the Gibb River Road, the Anne Beadell Highway or even the Canning Stock Route, you will always find corrugations in the road. There has been much conjecture over time as to what causes corrugations but suffice to say—the more traffic the road receives and the less maintenance applied to it, the worse the corrugations will be. I'm sure everyone has encountered corrugations at some stage and found they are difficult to negotiate due to the vibrations they cause in the vehicle and the loss of traction they create. A series of corrugations on a corner can see your vehicle skip sideways as you try to steer around the bend. Worse still, severe corrugations seem to shake and rattle not only everything in and on your vehicle but they also impact on the driver with the constant vibration. I am often amazed at the pounding that my vehicle can take on corrugated roads. Although, having said that, I would suggest that corrugations are the single most cause of damage to a vehicle via broken roof racks and ruined shock absorbers.

So, how do you drive a road that is corrugated? There is no simple answer, as the size of corrugations varies greatly, and their location on the road and prevailing conditions may make it difficult to drive over them at the ideal speed. I once followed a camel for five kilometres on the Anne Beadell Highway on severe corrugations. The camel was running at 40km/h and the closed-in bushes on each side of the track prevented the camel leaving the track. At 40km/h my Landcruiser was in and out of every corrugation and it was most certainly the wrong speed for this stretch of road. In the end I stopped and had lunch to allow the camel to get off the road.

If you encounter corrugations, firstly select four-wheel drive or, if you are able to activate your centre differential lock, then do so. Having proper four-wheel drive helps the vehicle grip the road despite

the poor grip conditions caused by the uneven road surface. It is also fair to say that you should attempt to drive at a speed that will see your tyres bounce from the top of each corrugation to the next one without actually travelling in and out of each depression synonymous with corrugations. By skipping the tyres over the top of the corrugations the shock absorbers are not working near as much in controlling the bounce of the vehicle and consequently continue to perform as designed. If you allow each tyre to ride up and down the corrugations then the shock absorber will be working flat out to control the spring movement—it is this rapid and intense movement that quickly over heats the internal oil of the shock absorber leading to decline in the shock absorber's efficiency. Continue driving like this and eventually your shock absorbers will fail totally, often in a dramatic way with them literally tearing themselves apart due to the massive friction built up in the shock absorber.

The speed necessary to skip across the top of corrugations will vary depending on the depth of the corrugation and the spacing between them. I've driven corrugated roads where 30km/h was suitable and others where 70km/h was necessary. Not everyone is comfortable with driving at higher speeds on corrugated roads but let me assure you—this is far more preferable than changing a set of ruined shock absorbers at a remote campsite in the desert.

My best advice is to find the speed that provides the smoothest possible ride for the vehicle. Whilst doing this, continue to look for the smoothest part of the

Driving the corrugated Mereenie Loop, Central Australia

track to drive on, choosing to drive where the height of the corrugations appears to be minimal. This may mean using all sections of the road, fortunately on our major roads such as the Tanami, Birdsville, Strzelecki and Oodnadatta Tracks you usually have sufficient forward vision to see any oncoming traffic well in advance. But never place your vehicle on the wrong side of the road on blind corners or crests.

Finally, sometimes it just isn't possible to find that perfect speed (the abandoned Gunbarrel Highway comes to mind) and you have to drive slowly, in and out of each corrugation. Do this at a much reduced speed and stop regularly to allow your shock absorbers to cool down.

passing oncoming traffic

On straight, unsealed roads stay in the centre of the road unless you see an approaching vehicle. Slow down and then move well to the left approximately 100 metres before the vehicle. In fact, the slower you go when you pass an oncoming vehicle the less chance there is of your windscreen sustaining damage from flying stones. Even if the other driver does not slow down, you should. Get as far away from the speeding vehicle as possible and come almost to a stop, otherwise a cracked windscreen is very likely.

If a road train is encountered travelling in the opposite direction on an unsealed road, the best advice is to actually pull off the road and stop. Wait until the road train has passed and the enormous dust cloud has cleared before proceeding. It is my experience that there are often two or three road trains travelling in convoy and you should be aware that there may be more than one approaching you in that dust cloud. The road train drivers cannot move their giant rigs off the centre of the road—so please do not think they are being road hogs by not moving over, they will appreciate it more if you move over and stop well clear of the road. Another tip with road trains; the drivers often talk to each other using channel 40 (UHF). Or, use your radio's scan feature if you have it, you will soon find what channel they are using. By either eavesdropping or politely interrupting their conversation you will find out how many trucks are in their convoy.

overtaking in dusty conditions

Overtaking other vehicles on unsealed roads is a tricky task. If you find that you are catching another vehicle on this type of road it is best to close your vehicle's air vents and put the air conditioner onto re-circulate; this will help to keep the dust out of the interior. However, do not constantly sit in the dust of another vehicle. Your four-wheel drive will be sucking dust-laden air into its air filter. This can quickly clog your air filter which will lead to loss of power and very high fuel consumption. In extreme circumstances, the abrasive dust can pass through the air filter and into your engine. This will lead to premature failure of your engine.

If following another vehicle in dusty conditions, put your headlights on; this will help passing traffic to see you. Try to contact the vehicle ahead on the UHF radio to ask if they could advise when it is safe to overtake. If this is not possible and you are obviously travelling faster than the other vehicle, approach cautiously from behind. It is very difficult in dusty conditions for you to even see the road surface, let alone avoid bad ruts or potholes.

Attempt to overtake only when you are certain it is safe to do so and keep well to the right, but try to avoid placing your tyres in the loose stones on the shoulder of the road. Remember that the driver of the vehicle you are overtaking may not know that you are there. The driver of the other vehicle is concentrating on the road ahead, does not expect there to be other users on this lonely road and cannot see anything behind his or her vehicle due

to the excessive dust. In these circumstances it is common for the driver ahead of you to suddenly cut you off as he or she weaves to avoid rough surfaces on the road. Use your horn and lights to try to alert the other driver that you are overtaking. If the other driver has any common sense, he or she will slow down and let you go. Common sense dictates that the slower driver should slow down and let you go, but human nature means the reverse often occurs. If it is too dangerous to pass, it is time for you to stop, have a tea break and wait a few minutes, letting the other driver get ahead and out of the way for a while.

wheel ruts

At times you will encounter deep wheel ruts on these relatively good roads. These are caused by other vehicles using the roads when they are wet. As the sun dries the road

surface, deep wheel ruts are left and baked rock-hard. These roads should be driven slowly to avoid the ruts throwing the vehicle around and possibly causing a roll over. You may also find that the mounds of earth between the ruts are so high that they scrape underneath your four-wheel drive. These mounds can contain rocks or very hard clay sections which could cause damage to the undercarriage or tyres. Avoid the deepest ruts by driving either side of them. A reduced speed is best used as you will need to frequently change direction moving from one side of the road to the other looking for the smoothest section of the road.

bull dust

Another hazard on the typical outback Australian road is bull dust. Bull dust is formed by the constant passage of trucks, four-wheel drives and

other vehicles over soft sections of the unsealed road. The ground breaks down into fine dust which at times can hide deep holes and long ruts in the road surface.

To negotiate these bull dust holes safely, you need to know where they are. If you cannot identify that the track ahead has a large bull dust area, adjust your driving style—it is highly likely that damage may occur to your vehicle. A deep bull dust hole, hit at speed, can easily damage a wheel rim, burst a tyre and even, in some cases, result in the four-wheel drive rolling over.

The easiest way to recognise a potential section of bull dust is to note that there is a visual change to the road surface. As you approach a bull dust hole you should be able to see that the road surface appears to form waves running across the road. In fact these waves are wheel ruts or depressions left in the soft sand-like surface. The tops of the ruts are rounded and smooth, whereas a dry-packed wheel rut is sharp and quite distinct.

Once you have identified that the road surface ahead may have bull dust sections, you should slow down to approximately 20 or 30 km/h (less if the bull dust appears to be extremely deep). Quite often in areas where bull dust has formed you will find the road has been widened by other vehicles driving around the bull dust hole. Provided the road surface around these holes looks firm, and provided you are not creating a new track over vegetated or fragile areas, it is preferable to follow this course. If the bull dust section stretches across the road, slow down as mentioned earlier and then steer the vehicle straight through the hole. Try not to make sharp turning manoeuvres whilst in the dust and be prepared for a giant plume of dust to erupt behind the vehicle. The dust cloud may even envelope the whole four-wheel drive and you need to be prepared for momentary loss of forward vision. It may even be necessary to apply the windscreen wipers to clear the soft dust which settles on the vehicle. Do not drive through these bull dust holes with your windows or your air vents open. The vehicle will easily fill with choking dust if you ignore this advice. Even if your vehicle is well-sealed against the entry of dust, the bull dust will leave a fine film of powder-like dust throughout the four-wheel drive.

In long and deep sections of bull dust the use of four-wheel drive may be necessary to avoid being bogged. Select high range four-wheel drive and first or second gear depending on the depth and length of the bull dust. Drive the vehicle on the throttle through the hole.

If travelling in prolonged dusty conditions, the vehicle's air filter can easily become clogged with dust. In these circumstances the performance of the vehicle will drop and the fuel usage will increase dramatically. It is a good habit to check your air filter each day when travelling on dusty roads and clean it if necessary.

tyre pressures

There are as many stories about tyre pressures for four-wheel drives as there are books written on four-wheel drive travel. From many years of outback touring, both for pleasure and conducting four-wheel drive tag-along tours, I have found that without question it is high tyre pressures that create most punctures on unsealed roads. On the typical unsealed road where speeds up to 100 km/h are possible, you should not exceed 40psi (pounds per square inch) in your tyres. Even if you are carrying a heavy load and have been advised to inflate the tyres to a high pressure for highway work, when you hit the unsealed sections keep your pressures below 40psi. I use 34psi on my Landcruiser when it is fully loaded for an outback safari and have suffered very few punctures.

wet tracks in the outback

The outback is an exciting place to visit in a four-wheel drive. The beauty and isolation lend

themselves to four-wheel drive touring. Careful selection of the time you travel in the outback is of the utmost importance. Do not contemplate outback four-wheel drive journeys during the summer months as the extreme temperatures can make this a very hazardous exercise. Similarly, travel in the wet season (which corresponds with the hot weather), is also very restricted due to flooded roads and the possibility of being stranded for days or weeks on end.

As a result, most of what we term outback travel occurs in the winter and spring months. At this time of the year, if travelling north of the Tropic of Capricorn, the chances of rain are virtually nil. In fact, it is these endless days of clear blue skies that attract many people to the Top End in winter. The tracks are basically dry and dusty. However, it is not the same south of the Tropic of Capricorn. Even though it is still known as the dry season, there is certainly an increased chance of wet weather across Central Australia; the southern sections of Western Australia and Queensland; most of New South Wales, Victoria, South Australia and Tasmania. Having travelled extensively throughout the outback during the winter months over the past 30 years, I would estimate that the chance of striking rain south of the Tropic of Capricorn at this time can be as high as 40%.

Now, whilst this rain may only fall for a few hours and rarely for a couple of days, it can cause untold havoc to any unsealed roads. If you are caught somewhere off the sealed road when rain falls you will quickly realise how suddenly a track surface can change.

The golden rule with wet roads in the outback is to establish whether the road is in fact open or closed. It is an offence to drive on a road that has been closed due to wet weather and hefty fines apply to those who disregard this advice. The damage caused to a wet road by the passing of a four-wheel drive can be huge. The cost of having hundreds of kilometres of unsealed road graded because of the inconsiderate actions of a tourist is very high.

You can identify closed roads by either observing ROAD CLOSED signs placed across the road by local authorities; the sign boards located outside major service areas indicating the condition of roads ahead; or by calling the local police and seeking their advice. Most state government road authorities provide

recorded road condition information on free call numbers. Travellers in remote areas should be carrying either a HF radio (Flying Doctor Radio) or a satellite telephone, along with the relevant contact numbers and details, so that contact can be made to ascertain this information.

If a road is closed you must not use it or, if you are already on a road that becomes closed due to wet weather, you should make camp and wait until the road is re-opened or as otherwise directed by a police officer or relevant authority. As the road user, it is your responsibility to be aware of whether the road is open or not. For this reason everyone travelling in the outback should carry extra food and water. I have known roads around Central Australia to be closed for up to seven days during the peak tourist season. Therefore, adequate supplies for an

enforced stay of at least seven days would be a good idea.

So how do you drive on a wet outback road that is not closed? There will be times when the roads are open but they are still wet. This can lead to one of the most memorable four-wheel drive experiences you are ever likely to have. It can also end in disaster if you are not careful.

Most outback roads are generally flat. The same outback road that only hours earlier was developing giant plumes of dust as you sped over it will suddenly become a sloppy mess of red clinging clay. It is amazing how quickly a road can become slippery with even the slightest shower of rain. The plus side is that there is no more dust; the down side, there is very little traction. Your tyres will quickly clog up with mud, making traction virtually impossible. Any tyre that has a non-aggressive tread pattern will be like a racing slick and provide as much traction as an ice cube on an ice rink. The more aggressive mud terrain tyres do help in these conditions but they too will find the going tough.

Once the tyre has clogged with mud the ability to get traction is severely limited. The use of four-wheel drive is mandatory. If you have the choice of locking your four-wheel drive's centre differential, then this should be done. With the vehicle in true four-wheel drive you should use high range. Depending on how slippery the track is; a speed of not more than 20 or 30 km/h should be maintained.

You will find that you are required to constantly correct the steering as the four-wheel drive waltzes down the track. It will constantly slide from one side to the other. Steer into the direction of the slide as it occurs. Do not brake suddenly nor make sudden or sharp steering adjustments. Your driving style needs to be gentle and subtle. The old adage of steering into the slide certainly applies, but do not accelerate if the vehicle has obviously lost traction and is sliding sideways. You should lift your foot off the accelerator allowing the motor to retard progress. Do not use the brakes as this will only lock the wheels. Once traction has been regained you can gently apply the accelerator and steer back towards the centre of the road.

Most outback roads are 'crowned' or graded in a curve shape across the road. This allows water to run off the crown of the road providing a slightly drier surface on which to drive. However, this crowning effect can make it very difficult to keep the four-wheel drive on the top of the crown. Once you slide to the left or the right of the crown or the more level section of the road, you will find that gravity and the loss of traction will work against you. The four-wheel drive will tend to slide off the crown of the road and head for the table drain beside the road. This can be potentially very bad as once you lose control altogether and slide into the table drain beside the road you are exposing your vehicle to much wetter and deeper mud in the drain. This could even result in a possible roll over or severe bogging where a culvert intersects the table drain.

In these circumstances the faster you drive the more chance there is of sliding right off the road. Slow down and maintain a speed that keeps your four-wheel drive on the top of the road's crown. Steering corrections into each sideways movement will still be needed.

If travelling with friends in a convoy keep your distance on this type of road. If you get too close there will not be sufficient space for you to take evasive action if the front vehicle slides off the road. Also, your close presence to the vehicle in front can make that driver nervous which results in them driving faster than they should in such conditions. Allow at least 100 metres between each vehicle. Radio communication between vehicles can be very handy, with the lead vehicle warning of particularly slippery sections or potential trouble spots. UHF radio is recommended for this purpose.

Water will often pool across a wet road and it is best to assess whether there are deep ruts in the pooled water and avoid these if you can. But be very wary of steering around the pools of water as the surface away from the graded road section will be even boggier and the chances of becoming stranded on the edge of the road are very real.

Before entering the pool of water activate your windscreen wipers as the brown/red muddy water will cascade over the windscreen as you plough through the puddle. Reduce speed to no more than 30 km/h and less if the water is more than ankle deep otherwise you run the risk of pushing water into your radiator fan and causing radiator damage or into the air intake causing engine damage.

The mud can build-up under the vehicle quite quickly and I have known wheel arches to become completely laden with mud. At times it may even be necessary to stop the vehicle and clear the mud from wheel arches to permit the wheels to keep turning. Carry a small spade for this purpose.

The mud and grit-laden water can play havoc with your vehicle's electrics, especially the alternator. If you have driven through an excessive amount of mud it is wise to have the vehicle's vital components checked by a four-wheel drive mechanic once you get home or sooner. This includes checking your alternator, wheel bearings and differentials for possible water entry. Brake pads can fill with the clingy red mud which contains small abrasive stones and it is quite common for brake pads to literally wear away in a few hundred kilometres. Check

brakes and clean them as soon as you leave the muddy track.

At the same time it is a good idea to clear the excess build-up of mud off your inner and outer wheel rims. Once this mud dries it can set like concrete and will almost certainly affect the wheel balance of each rim.

When driving a vehicle with an automatic transmission on wet outback roads, it is a good idea for you to select the gear that you wish to be in. Do not just leave the transmission in DRIVE as this will not give you the engine braking and throttle response that you would have if you select your desired gear ratio. Naturally these vehicles will also have four-wheel drive high range engaged with the centre differential locked where fitted.

Some automatic vehicles also offer the choice of second gear starting. This is used in very slippery conditions when the amount of power fed to the wheels is too great and wheel spin is easily encouraged. By selecting the second gear start option on the transmission there is less torque fed to the wheels and more chance of them gaining traction. Use this facility if you stop on a very muddy surface and have trouble gaining traction again.

Turning corners in wet conditions where the red clay or black soil is like a skating rink can be a character building exercise. The driver will find very little reaction to the steering as the vehicle tends to oversteer straight ahead. I remember a memorable drive out from Haddon Corner on a very wet track.

flooded claypan

To negotiate corners on the road it was necessary to commence sliding the four-wheel drive several metres before the corner and then turn the steering into the slide as the corner was approached. This made the vehicle follow the course of the road through the bend. Then it was a process of sliding the vehicle in the opposite direction and steering into that slide to straighten up the vehicle for the exit of the corner. If you were lucky, the vehicle safely negotiated the curve. If not, it meant a recovery exercise from the side of the road. It took a whole day to drive 60 kilometres using this technique (and rescuing those vehicles that got it wrong). So I guess the lesson here is to always carry vehicle recovery equipment just in case.

safety in the outback

Remember you're a long way from home and help when you get out past the black stump—so always drive cautiously. I'm sure you would prefer to enjoy your holiday and come home with lots of great memories rather than spend a week broken down in a small country town, or see your means of transport carted off on the back of a tilt tray tow truck.

Always look for obstacles on unsealed roads, drive at a speed that allows you to stop or take evasive action without losing control, drive with your headlights on so you are clearly visible to all traffic (both oncoming and passing), stop regularly to check your vehicle for tyre condition, oil or water leaks and loose shock absorbers or other accessories on the vehicle. If you see a problem, attend to it, a small leak from a radiator will quickly develop into a

major problem on unsealed roads where there may be little help.

Carry spare parts for your vehicle, especially air filters, fuel filters, fan belts and radiator hoses. Carry basic tools to help you change these components. Carry a means of communication, satellite telephone or HF radio (in remote locations) and always carry spare water and some food.

Rain can make outback roads impassable

stranded in the outback

If you become bogged or breakdown then there are a few do's and don'ts that you should remember.

do:

- Do always carry a satellite phone and Personal Locating Beacon.

- Do always tell someone where you are going and when you should be there and ensure they know to follow it up if you have not checked in.

- Do carry extra water and food and use it sparingly but sensibly.

- Do know how your four-wheel drive operates, many people have perished because they did not know how to correctly engage four-wheel drive.

- Do stay with your vehicle, never try to walk out, most people perish in the outback by leaving their vehicle and exposing themselves to extreme heat or cold. By staying with the vehicle you have a greater chance of being found as the vehicle is more easily seen by rescue parties

- Do stay in the shade of the vehicle during the heat of the day, make shade using a tarpaulin or tent off the side of your vehicle

don't:

- Don't Panic. Think about your predicament and check that you have engaged four-wheel drive

- Don't leave the vehicle.

- Don't try to walk out to get help unless you know for certain it is less than 30 minutes away, i.e. you saw an occupied homestead. If in doubt stay with your vehicle.

- Don't try to dig out the four-wheel drive if bogged, in the hot sun you will dehydrate very quickly, wait until the cool of the evening to do any strenuous activity

- Don't drink any alcohol, it dehydrates you even more.

chapter 10

SUGGESTED ITINERARIES

To assist you with your planning I have described below some basic itineraries for various periods of time. This will give you a rough guide of what can be achieved.

where to go in one week

If located on the east coast of Australia one week won't get you into the Outback so aim for a more local trip.

- Out of Brisbane the most obvious location would be a run up to the beautiful Fraser Island or down to the four-wheel drive locations around Coffs Harbour and through to Tamworth where there are some great bush camps in rainforest areas of Werrikimbe National Park and the Oxley Wild Rivers National Park.

- For a week out of Sydney you can explore outback New South Wales with a

Flinders Ranges

drive through Willandra National Park, Mungo National Park, then follow the Darling River to Menindee Lakes and Mutawintji National Park north of Broken Hill.

- From Melbourne the most obvious one week escape in summer is into the magnificent High Country which stretches from just north of Sale all the way to the New South Wales border at Khancoban covering such iconic locations as Howitt High Plains, Grant Historic Area, Dargo, Wonnangatta Valley, Craig's Hut and the Davies High Plains area north of Benambra.

- For a week out of Adelaide a visit into the magnificent Flinders Ranges is suggested, visit the well known Wilpena Pound and Brachina Gorge; and make sure you take time to explore the many private station tracks such as Willow Springs.

Mungo National Park

- From Perth I would suggest heading east to the beautiful beaches around Esperance and Cape Le Grand National Park, and of course in spring a loop out to Kalgoorlie via the wildflower scenic route is a must.

where to go in two weeks

- From all the major capital cities you now have the opportunity to cross one of Australia's most famous deserts, the Simpson Desert. The Simpson Desert is absolutely beautiful, and will draw you back time and time again.

- For east coasters; head west to Broken Hill, and then onto Marree, via the main road to get out there as quickly as possible. From Marree you can slow your pace as you trace the route of the Old Ghan Railway up the Oodnadatta Track. There is a wealth of interesting, scenic and historic sites to see along the Oodnadatta Track, and as a minimum allow two days to travel from Marree

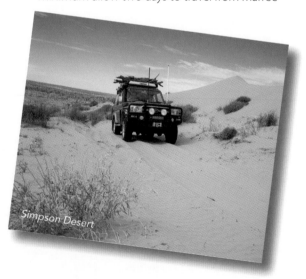

Simpson Desert

to the Pink Roadhouse at Oodnadatta. This may be your last refuelling point before entering the desert, unless you continue up the track to Blood Creek and onto the isolated Mt Dare Station which has good campsites, cool ale and expensive fuel.

- From the west coast around Perth, it's a relatively easy run up the Great Central Highway from Laverton to Uluru. You will need a permit to transit this area but they are easily obtained. This will take about four days of solid driving. Take the opportunity to check out Uluru before slipping across the sealed highway to Kulgera, and then hitting the gravel once more into Finke. This will take a couple of days with another day to reach the edge of the Simpson Desert at Mt Dare.

- Our Adelaide and South Australian friends can head straight up, possibly the most boring road in Australia, the Stuart Highway from Port Augusta to Coober Pedy. Then enjoy wandering through the Painted Desert on their way to Oodnadatta before heading to Mt Dare, or straight into the desert via Dalhousie Springs. Alternatively, South Australians can make a real journey of the trip to the desert and pass through the beautiful Gammon Ranges, around Lake Gairdner and then up to Kingoonya on the Trans Australian Railway, before heading to Oodnadatta and then onto Mt Dare.

Simpson Desert

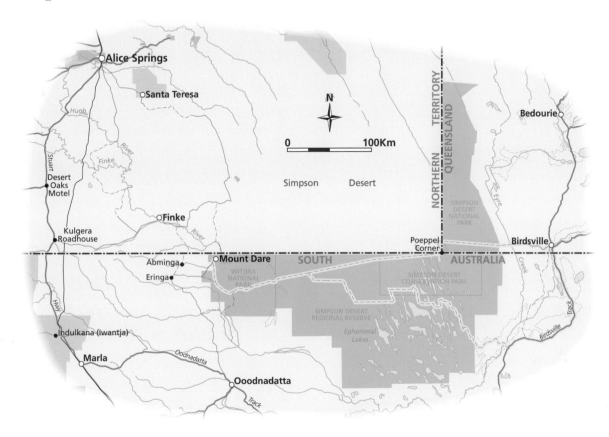

big red

- **From Mt Dare:**
  - You head east into the desert with a stop at the Dalhousie Thermal Springs, an absolute must, for a swim in the 38 degrees Celsius water, and an inspection of the old ruins nearby.
- You need to allow a minimum of three days to cross the thousand plus parallel sand dunes across the dead heart of Australia. You will need to: drop your tyre pressures; be self-sufficient for the crossing; able to fix anything that fails; and carry upwards of 200 litres of fuel.

French Line - Simpson Desert

- This leads to the most iconic town in Australia, Birdsville, where you can camp by the Diamantina River or sleep in three star luxury accommodation at the hotel.

- The trip home can be via the historic Dig Tree near Innamincka, made famous by the fateful journey of Burke and Wills.
- East coasters can then head home via the Strzelecki Track or Cameron Corner, Tibooburra and White Cliffs.
- South Australians can take their time heading home as they explore Arkaroola and the Flinders Ranges.
- West Australians will have a rushed trip back via the Eyre Highway and the Nullabor Plain, but if you have a few extra days there are some great sights along here; with excellent sand driving at Fowlers Bay, the fantastic Head of Bight whale watching area and even a four-wheel drive track to follow from Madura to the Eyre Bird Observatory.

where to go in four weeks

- For east coasters from Melbourne to Brisbane a prime location might be to Cape York.
- It takes almost a week just to drive on the highway from Melbourne to Cairns and two weeks is the minimum amount of time you need to have a good look around the Cape, three or four is better. Cape York is still on the must see list of most outback travellers, but it is definitely four-wheel drive country. Although, the main Telegraph Road north of Weipa, is the easier route, there are plenty of side tracks to scenic locations such as Chilli Beach and Captain Billy Landing that you will wish to explore.

Cape York

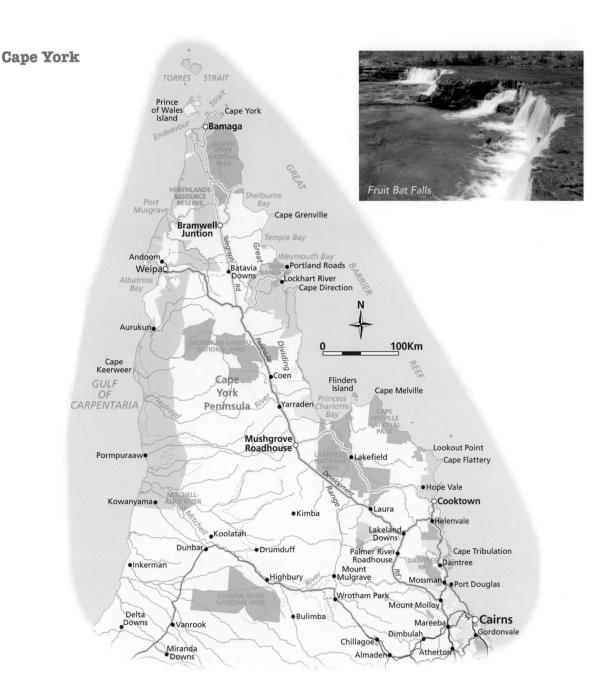

TORRES STRAIT

Endeavour Strait

Prince of Wales Island

Cape York

Bamaga

JARDINE RIVER NATIONAL PARK

GREAT

HEATHLANDS RESOURCE RESERVE

Port Musgrave

Shelburne Bay

Cape Grenville

Bramwell Juntion

Telegraph Rd.

Great

Temple Bay

Weymouth Bay

Andoom

IRON RANGE NP

Portland Roads

Weipa

Batavia Downs

Lockhart River

Cape Direction

Albatross Bay

BARRIER

N

Aurukun

MUNGKAN KANDJU NATIONAL PARK

Peninsula

Dividing

0   100Km

Cape Keerweer

Cape York Peninsula

Coen

Flinders Island

Cape Melville

REEF

GULF OF CARPENTARIA

Holroyd

River

Princess Charlotte Bay

CAPE MELVILLE NATIONAL PARK

Yarraden

Pormpuraaw

Mushgrove Roadhouse

LAKEFIELD NATIONAL PARK

Lakefield

Lookout Point

Cape Flattery

MITCHELL-ALICE RIVER NP

Hope Vale

Kowanyama

Mitchell

Development

Range

Kimba

Laura

Cooktown

Helenvale

Koolatah

Drumduff

Lakeland Downs

Dunbar

Palmer River Roadhouse

Cape Tribulation

DAINTREE NP

Daintree

Inkerman

Mount Mulgrave

Rd.

Mossman

Port Douglas

Highbury

River

Wrotham Park

Mount Molloy

Delta Downs

STAATEN RIVER NATIONAL PARK

Bulimba

Mareeba

Cairns

Vanrook

Dimbulah

Gordonvale

Miranda Downs

Chillagoe

Almaden

Atherton

Fruit Bat Falls

Old Telegraph Track - Cape York

- Four weeks also allows time for both east and west coast residents to visit the Red Centre. A great itinerary for this trip is:

- Travel along the Oodnadatta Track, following the Old Ghan Railway through Finke up to Chambers Pillar. Then continue north, where a visit to Rainbow Valley at sunset is a must do item, as is a few days in Alice Springs—there is so much to see in the Alice.

- A drive to the east of Alice Springs via Ross River homestead, Arltunga and then up the Cattlewater Pass Track to Gemtree can be followed by a similar loop to the west of Alice Springs to all the beautiful gorges including Simpson Gap, Ellery Creek, Ormiston Gorge and Glen Helen Gorge. Then a visit to Palm Valley, followed by the magnificent four-wheel drive route south along the bed of the Finke River to Boggy Hole and onto Kings Canyon is not to be missed. Take a full day to explore the magnificent

- The roads are corrugated may have deep bull dust sections and there are numerous rivers and creeks to be crossed that can and still trap unwary drivers. Of course there is the ever present danger of crocodiles too!

Chambers Pillar

Finke River bed near Boggy Hole

Red Centre

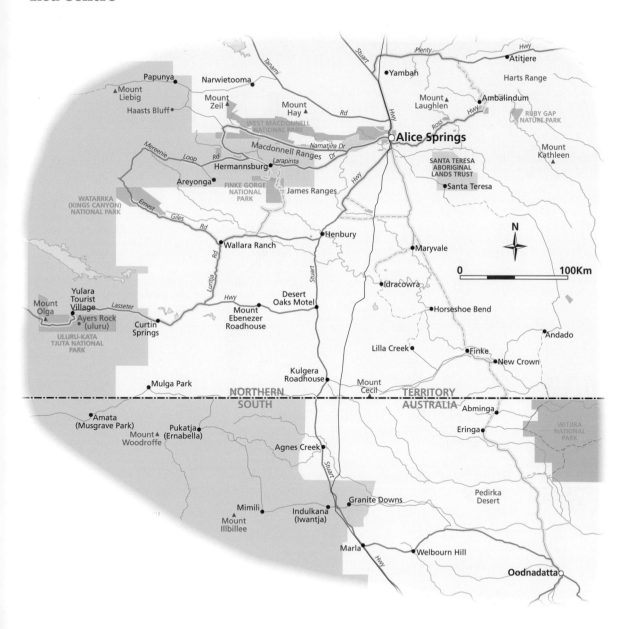

The Lambert Centre, the geographical centre of Australia

Ghost Gum, East MacDonnell Ranges, Red Centre

Kings Canyon, before the mandatory drive south to Uluru to witness sunset and sunrise on the most famous monolith in the country.

- Those living on the west coast will have the opportunity to explore the amazing coastal scenery to the north of Perth and combine it with a visit to one of the most outstanding locations I have ever seen, Karijini National Park.

- Heading north of Perth, if you haven't seen the fascinating landscape around Cervantes known as the Pinnacles, now is a good time. From here follow the coast road up to the bustling city of Geraldton and stop off at the beautiful monument to HMAS Sydney. A little further north is the coast road that leads you out to Kalbarri passing the pink waters of Hutt Lagoon. The coast at Kalbarri deserves a day or two to explore with its many bays and high cliffs. But the real attraction at Kalbarri is the national park with its sculptured rock formations such as Nature's Window and the deeply gouged gorge country created by the meandering Murchison River.

- The next port of call for the four-wheel drive enthusiast would be the sandy and limestone rock drive out to the most westerly point of Australia, Steep Point. This is a fabulous trip and the huge cliffs at Steep Point are equalled in grandeur by the beautiful azure coloured waters that lap the sandy beaches of Denham Sound. On the other side of sound you have the world famous Monkey Mia with its controlled feeding programs for the resident dolphins. But, if you

Karijini National Park

want a true wilderness experience without the crowds and regulations, head up to Francois Peron National Park where white sands and red rocks merge with the blue waters to form one of the most scenically attractive places on earth.

- Further up the coast you have large citrus growing areas around Carnarvon fed by the waters of the Gascoyne River and then at Coral Bay the Ningaloo Reef is close enough to the shoreline to view from glass bottom boats or whilst snorkelling in the crystal clear waters. A sandy four-wheel drive track leads past the old Ningaloo Station to the often deep crossing of Yardie Creek where you can take a boat cruise to view the rocky cliffs carved into the coast. Sealed roads lead past amazing beaches to the crowded settlement of Exmouth. You should

Pinnacles, Nambung National Park, Western Australia

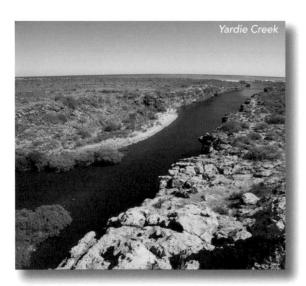
Yardie Creek

twisted rock strata of Hamersley Gorge and the view from Mt Nameless is almost as good as that from Mt Sheila.

- Now head into Karijini National Park making your base camp at Dales Camp above the Fortescue Falls. You will need at least three days here to walk all the incredible gorges, Dales, Weano and Hancock, to name a few. This is one of the most scenic spots in Australia and everyone must get to see Karijini National Park at some stage in their life. It does require a fair degree of fitness as all the gorges require walking, but each of the lookouts are easily accessible by motor vehicle and they are equally stunning.

- Your time has all but gone so make your way home via Newman stopping off for the two hour tour of the huge open cut mine. From here the Northern Highway heads south to Meekatharra and Mt Magnet where you can head back across to the coast or continue south west to Perth through the wildflower centre of Western Australia.

allow a few days on this coastal strip, you can even camp on the edge of the beach in your own private sandy site.

- It's another days drive up the highway to Karratha where you can get your permit from the Visitor's Centre to drive the Hamersley Iron railway service road. Now for a trip through some of the most stunning country in Australia. The railway service road leads to Millstream Chichester National Park, stop off at Python Pool and wonder at the piles of red rocks seemingly dumped at random by a giant dump truck. You can camp beside the Fortescue River (no wood fires) and enjoy the tranquil waters of this large waterway. You will marvel at the 240 carriage ore trains as you continue east to Tom Price, but make sure you take the side trip to Mt Sheila where you will see the most breathtaking view ever. From Tom Price its an easy run out to the

Mt Nameless WA

Turquoise Bay, Cape Range National Park, WA

- The Canning Stock Route is possibly the most demanding four-wheel drive trip in the world. It is the absolute isolation that makes it so, combined with the endurance needed by both vehicle and driver. To embark on a trip along the Canning Stock Route you really need to be well prepared for remote area travel and be self-sufficient. This self-sufficiency extends to being able to fix mechanical issues that may beset you as well as carry all your food supplies for at least two weeks and possibly a lot longer. Water is available at some of the old historic wells, but you still need to carry at least 80 litres. Fuel is another problem, there are not many reliable fuel outlets along the route. It is possible to arrange a fuel drop at Well 23 through the Capricorn Roadhouse in Newman or there may be fuel available at the Kunawarritji community near Well 33. However, to even reach these locations you require large quantities of fuel up to 250 litres of diesel and up to 350 litres of petrol if you are driving a large V8 powered petrol four-wheel drive.

- The driving conditions are difficult with a mix of rocky tracks and soft sand. There are hundreds of sand dunes with soft ridges and uneven surfaces that prevent high speed approaches. It is common to average just 20kph all day in these conditions. Corrugations are found throughout the 2000 kilometre length of the CSR and these alone can cause more damage to your four-wheel drive than any other road condition encountered. Suspension in particular takes a pounding and carrying spare shock absorbers is a must. Roof racks suffer too and often break with the heavy loads and constant vibrations, so knowing how to bush weld with a couple of car batteries is virtually mandatory.

- Hopefully I have not scared you off doing this incredible four-wheel drive trip. The scenery along the CSR is ever changing with rocky outcrops, followed by vast dry salt lakes, towering red ochre cliffs, beautiful secluded valleys and the endless spinifex plains with the rolling sand dunes. Each crest of a sand dune brings a new vista from dark red sand to lush green valleys with stately desert oaks whispering in the outback breeze. The Aboriginal people called this home long before white man and evidence of their occupation is found in many rock art sites along the track. Access is controlled these days and you need your permit to enter

Well 46, Canning Stock Route

Canning Stock Route

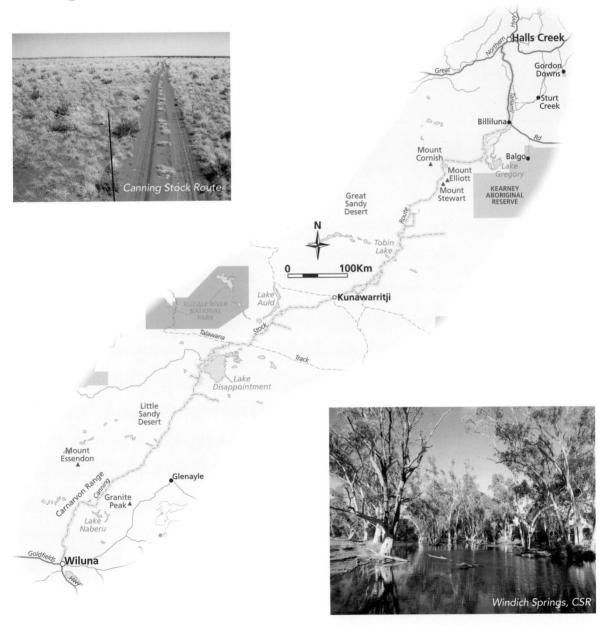

Canning Stock Route

N

0 100Km

Windich Springs, CSR

camping at Durba Springs

the Martu Land which is available via the Australian National 4WD Council, see permits in References & Resources on page 212.

- Many people travel the full length of the CSR either staring with Well 1 just outside the town of Wiluna in Western Australia or descending from the north from Well 51 near the Tanami Track not far from the community at Billiluna. As mentioned you need at least 14 days and if you are like me and prefer to take your time and explore places such as Durba Springs and the Breaden Hills you will need 20 or more days to complete the full trek. Remember, throughout this extensive period you need to be virtually self-sufficient. Some say it is the greatest four-

wheel drive trip you can do, you won't get any argument from me.

where to go in six weeks

- This is an ideal time for anyone to venture north, either; to the Gulf of Carpentaria and then onto Darwin/Kakadu, or to the Kimberley Region.
- Travelling through The Gulf of Carpentaria onto Kakadu and Darwin, offers some spectacular scenery and driving:
- East coasters might take a route through Central Queensland, allowing visits to well known locations as: Longreach home to the Stockman's Hall of Fame; Winton and the nearby Lark Quarry where a dinosaur stampede occurred; Boulia home of the mysterious Min Min lights; and then into the Gulf Country where you will find amazing gorge country of Lawn Hill National Park.

Gulf country

Gulf of Carpentaria

Purple Pub, Normanton

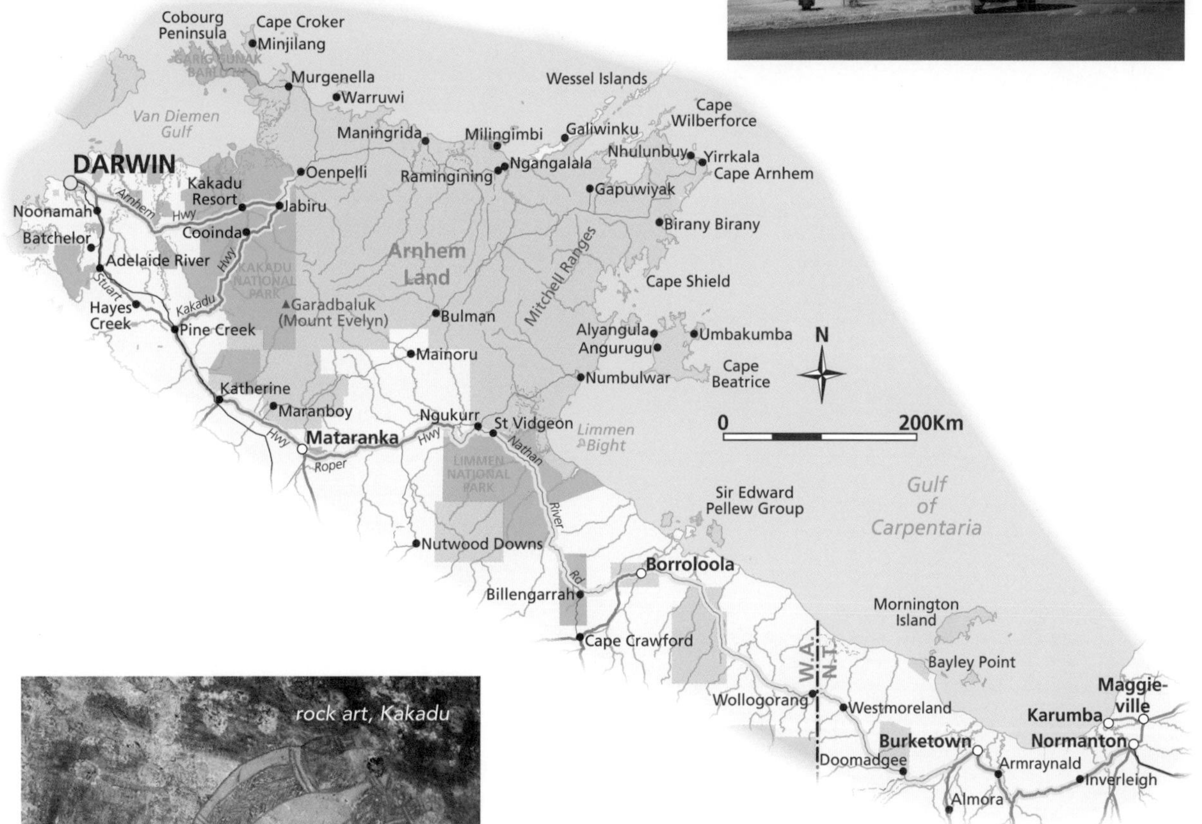

Cobourg Peninsula
Minjilang
Cape Croker
DARLUK BARLUK
Van Diemen Gulf
Murgenella
Warruwi
Wessel Islands
Cape Wilberforce
DARWIN
Maningrida
Milingimbi
Galiwinku
Nhulunbuy
Yirrkala
Cape Arnhem
Oenpelli
Ngangalala
Ramingining
Gapuwiyak
Kakadu Resort
Jabiru
Arnhem Hwy
Birany Birany
Noonamah
Batchelor
Cooinda
Arnhem Land
Adelaide River
KAKADU NATIONAL PARK
Cape Shield
Hayes Creek
Garadbaluk (Mount Evelyn)
Bulman
Alyangula
Angurugu
Umbakumba
Pine Creek
Kakadu
Mitchell Ranges
Mainoru
Cape Beatrice
N
Katherine
Numbulwar
Maranboy
Ngukurr
St Vidgeon
Limmen Bight
MATARANKA
Roper
Nathan
LIMMEN NATIONAL PARK
0   200Km
Sir Edward Pellew Group
Gulf of Carpentaria
Nutwood Downs
River Rd
Borroloola
Billengarrah
Mornington Island
Cape Crawford
Bayley Point
W.A. N.T.
Maggie-ville
Wollogorang
Westmoreland
Karumba
Normanton
Burketown
Doomadgee
Armraynald
Inverleigh
Almora

rock art, Kakadu

- Whilst people from South Australia can meander up the Stuart Highway pausing at Uluru and Kings Canyon before visiting Alice Springs and continuing north up the highway to Mataranka.

- Western Australians with their heart set on a visit to the Gulf/Savannah and Darwin need to rush across the Nullabor Plain and straight up the Stuart Highway to Mataranka.

- A drive across the Savannah Way from Karumba to Mataranka, or vice versa, will take you through hostile and remote country just below the Gulf of Carpentaria. There are plenty of wild rivers to be crossed, bull dust holes and kilometre after kilometre of corrugations. Time your trip in spring and you may even witness the phenomenal natural occurrence of the Morning Glory (a mass of low lying cloud that sweeps

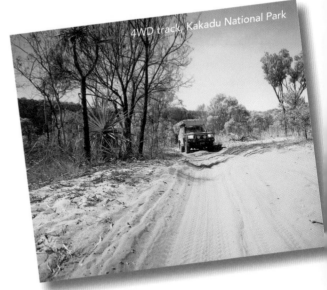

4WD track, Kakadu National Park

inland from the Gulf of Carpentaria like a huge rolling wave).

- Between the wild-west town of Borroloola and Mataranka on the Stuart Highway there are some of the most amazing rock formations to be seen. The Lost City at Cape Crawford is only accessible by helicopter, but others at Limmen National Park (the Southern Lost City and the Western Lost City) are just a short drive and walk from their respective car parks.

- Kakadu National Park has World Heritage listing and whilst it can be over run by tourists, if you are prepared to take the four-wheel drive tracks and do a little hiking you will soon realise why.

- Some say the Kimberley Region is the most beautiful place on earth and it is hard to argue with this statement.

Southern Lost City

Kimberley

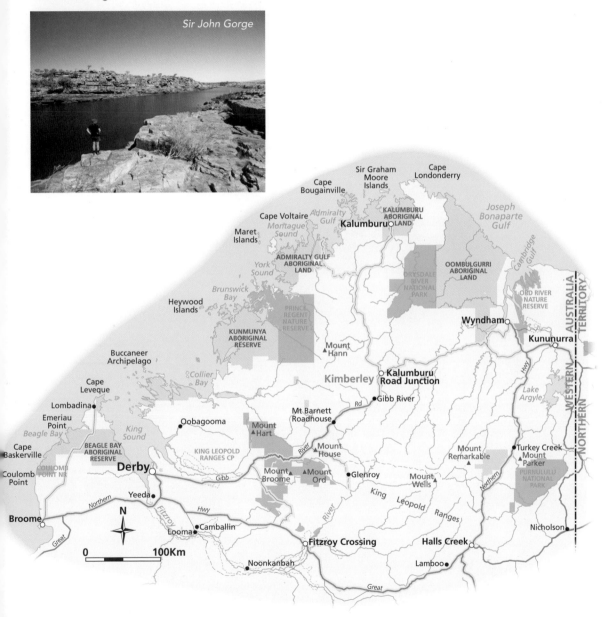

Sir John Gorge

Cape Londonderry

Sir Graham
Moore
Islands

Cape
Bougainville

*Joseph
Bonaparte
Gulf*

Cape Voltaire

*Admiralty
Gulf*

KALUMBURU
ABORIGINAL
LAND

*Montague
Sound*

Maret
Islands

Kalumburu

ADMIRALTY GULF
ABORIGINAL
LAND

*York
Sound*

DRYSDALE
RIVER
NATIONAL
PARK

OOMBULGURRI
ABORIGINAL
LAND

*Cambridge
Gulf*

*Brunswick
Bay*

ORD RIVER
NATURE
RESERVE

Heywood
Islands

PRINCE
REGENT
NATURE
RESERVE

KUNMUNYA
ABORIGINAL
RESERVE

Mount
Hann

Wyndham

Buccaneer
Archipelago

Kununurra

*Collier
Bay*

Kimberley

Kalumburu
Road Junction

AUSTRALIA

Cape
Leveque

Rd

Gibb River

*Lake
Argyle*

Lombadina

Mt Barnett
Roadhouse

Hwy

WESTERN

NORTHERN

TERRITORY

Emeriau
Point

Oobagooma

Mount
Hart

Beagle Bay

*King
Sound*

Mount
House

Cape
Baskerville

BEAGLE BAY
ABORIGINAL
RESERVE

River

Mount
Remarkable

Turkey Creek
Mount
Parker

Coulomb
Point

COULOMB
POINT NR

KING LEOPOLD
RANGES CP

Derby

Mount
Broome

Mount
Ord

Glenroy

Mount
Wells

PURNULULU
NATIONAL
PARK

Gibb

Yeeda

King

Leopold

Northern

Broome

Northern

Hwy

Looma

Camballin

Fitzroy

River

Ranges

Nicholson

N

Fitzroy Crossing

Halls Creek

Great

0   100Km

Noonkanbah

Lamboo

Great

Mitchell Falls - The Kimberley, Western Australia

- From Alice Springs it takes two long days of dusty driving up the Tanami Track where fuel supplies are your greatest concern. This leads to Halls Creek via the famous Wolfe Creek Crater. Around Halls Creek there are some great spots such as China Wall and Caroline Pool, as well as historic Old Halls Creek. But it is the massif known as Purnululu or the Bungle Bungle range that lies just north of the town that attracts tourist like bees to honey. This is a must visit location and you need two or three days as a minimum to see all the sights and soak in this spiritual place.

- Next stop is at the bustling town of Kununurra where you again need a few days to enjoy all that it offers. A cruise on the huge man-made Lake Argyle, or up the Ord River that was dammed to create the lake, or take a barramundi

Windjana Gorge

fishing safari out to the coast for fish tales that are true. You can even visit the famous Argyle Diamond Mine, the richest diamond mine in the world.

- From Kununurra its time to head into the heart of the Kimberley via Wyndham with its magnificent Five Rivers lookout and then travel the length of El Questro Station in the shadow of the Cockburn Range made famous in the film Australia. The scenery is far more stunning than that depicted in the movie. You can camp at El Questro and enjoy river cruises to see the Bradshaw art sites that pre date aboriginal art that is over 40 000 years old.

- Now its time to tackle the Gibb River Road with its amazing scenery, open river crossings and stony jump ups. This will lead you to the Mitchell Falls road one of the toughest in the Kimberley Region, but the reward of the view over the falls is worth every bone jarring corrugation. At the nearby Prince Regent River there is magnificent camping and more aboriginal art and burial sites. Further west along the Gibb River Road, you will see many gorges including Manning, Bell, Galvan's, Adcock and the crocodile infested (freshies) Windjana Gorge which lays at the base of a limestone reef .

- A visit to the Kimberley Region is not complete without taking the dusty and very scenic drive to the Mornington Wilderness Camp. Here you can canoe the mighty Fitzroy River at Dimond Gorge—the scenery is superb.

- Then onto Fitzroy Crossing where the road is sealed, and there are even shops. But the nearby Geikie Gorge is best seen from the guided boat cruises that operate all day in winter.

- Derby will be your first sight of the western waters that lap the crocodile infested mangroves, but it is Broome that is everyone's ultimate destination with its beautiful beaches, incredible sunsets and if you arrive on a full moon the amazing Stairway to the Moon—a natural phenomenon as the moon rises over the Roebuck Bay mud flats.

- To top off your Kimberley adventure head north from Broome to Cape Leveque, where you can laze on unspoilt beaches, stare in awe at the rich red rocks as the sun sets, or try your hand at catching the plentiful fish in the Hunter River.

- You will need to leave at least 10 days to get back home to the east coast via the Great Northern Highway, Tanami Track and the Stuart or Plenty Highways.

- Our South Australian and West Australian friends can follow a similar route after traversing the Stuart Highway to Alice Springs.

- West Australians are fortunate in that they can return home via the magnificent Western Australia coast from Broome to Geraldton.

- Also, the West Australian readers can plan their whole six weeks around exploring their own huge state with a run up the Canning Stock Route from Wiluna to Well 23 then follow the Talawana Track to the rugged beauty of Rudall River National Park, before exploring the outstanding scenic splendour of the Hamersley Ranges and returning home via the amazing coastal strip from Exmouth to Kalbarri.

i'm retired - what about me?

- With unlimited time, you can do all of the above trips. Even add in a trip to Tasmania, and the magnificent beaches and coastal scenery along the South Australian coastline.

- For our east coast friends this may be your best opportunity to thoroughly explore all of the scenic wonders of Western Australia including the spectacular Karijini National Park and the amazing white beaches and turquoise sea along the coast. Here is a suggested route:

- From Broome head south stopping at Barn Hill Station where there are incredible rock formations on the beach. Also stop at Eighty Mile Beach for fantastic

Ningaloo coastline

beach fishing. Continuing south, head inland into the mining country of Newman to view the biggest man-made hole in Australia. But, Karijini National Park, west of Newman, is the jewel in the crown of this region, and you will not fail to be impressed by the incredible colours of the Hamersley Range. You do need to be fit and energetic to really appreciate this park as there are numerous walks into deep canyons and narrow gorges with cool running streams to bathe in as you go. This is the most stunning place I have seen in Australia.

- From Karijini National Park, follow the giant rail line carrying the iron ore out to Dampier, and along the way stop in and visit Millstream-Chichester National Park. Then make your way down the magnificent west coast with visits to Exmouth and to Cape Arid National Park with the incredible white sand and blue sea around Yardie Creek. You can snorkel on the Ningaloo Reef at Coral Bay, view the world's oldest living organism (stromatolites) at Shark Bay near Monkey Mia, walk deserted beaches at Francois Peron National Park where dolphins frolic in the clear waters, and drive to the most westerly point of the Australian mainland at Steep Point.

- Continuing south there is the incredible rock formations of Kalbarri National Park, the petrified sentinels of Cervantes, and so much more to see as you follow the west coast all the way down to Perth and onwards to the magnificent karri forests and tree top walks at Pemberton.

For Western Australians on the big lap they now have time to thoroughly explore the east coast including:

- The High Country of Victoria with a through trip from Mansfield to Craig's Hut, over the range at Bluff Hut to the snow plains around Howitt's Hut, then down through the infamous Wonnangatta Valley and back over the next range to the gold mining area around Talbotville and Grant.

- From this magnificent mountain scenery keep heading north to Mt Hotham via the best four-wheel drive track in the country, Mt Blue Rag Range, and then take the Alpine Way to the quaint town of Omeo before heading north-east to the Davies High Plains via the very steep, low range, Limestone Creek Fire Trail.

Coolamine Homestead

- Continue on your mountain journey over the Davies High Plains and cross the mighty Murray River at Tom Groggin Station, and then head up to the highest town in Australia at Cabramurra.

- Follow the Elliot Way as it drops down through a gorge before reaching the top of the range, again, near Tumbarumba; where you can follow the powerline road. Here you will spot wild brumbies synonymous with the High Country before emerging back down in the river valley at Talbingo.

- You can continue your mountain journey via Long Plain and Coolamine Homestead and if travelling in summer even reach the Brindabella Ranges via Broken Cart Trail.

- A journey up the backbone of the Great Dividing Range is possible; travel via Mittagong and the ever descending and winding road to Wombeyan Caves before heading north to Oberon, and then up the Bridle Track from Bathurst to Hill End.

- From here you can cross through to the winery district of the Hunter Valley via Rylstone and Sandy Hollow, and once more climb the magnificent mountains over Barrington Tops.

- The journey continues along the mountains from Gloucester to Walcha up Thunderbolts Way, past the state's second highest waterfall, Wollomombi Falls, to the lush rainforests of New England National Park.

- The humidity rises as you follow the Waterfall Way through Dorrigo and over mountain roads past the whitewater rafting haven of the Nymboida River, before reaching the granite outcrops of Gibraltar Range National Park.

- From here it's not far to Queensland via the volcanic plug of Mt Warning and the amazing Scenic Rim around the Tweed Valley.

- More adventure of a different kind awaits you on Fraser Island. Then you can head inland to the incredible rock formations of Carnarvon Gorge and the underground Lava Tubes at Undara near Mount Surprise.

- From here you can explore Cape York and return home via the Savannah Way, Kakadu and Kimberley regions as described in the six week itinerary.

- What a fantastic country we have!

Exploring Fraser Island

Captain Billy Landing, Cape York, Queensland

Chilli Beach, Cape York, Queensland

chapter 11

YOUR OUTBACK PACKING LIST

vehicle equipment and spares

- ☐ Air filter
- ☐ Air conditioning belts
- ☐ Brake fluid
- ☐ Differential oil
- ☐ Engine oil (minimum 4 litres)
- ☐ Fan belt
- ☐ Fire extinguisher
- ☐ Front shock absorber
- ☐ Fuel filter
- ☐ Fuel hose
- ☐ Fuel pump
- ☐ Fuses
- ☐ Gearbox oil
- ☐ Hose clamps
- ☐ Inner tube
- ☐ Jerry can
- ☐ Radiator coolant
- ☐ Radiator hoses
- ☐ Rear shock absorber
- ☐ Self-tapping screws
- ☐ Shock rubbers (spare front & rear shock bushes)

- ☐ Spare globes
- ☐ Spare key
- ☐ Spare wheel rim
- ☐ Spare tyre
- ☐ Spark plugs (where applicable)
- ☐ Syringe oil pump
- ☐ Thermostat
- ☐ Transmission oil
- ☐ Water hoses
- ☐ Window chip repair kit
- ☐ Workshop manual

tools

- ☐ Air compressor
- ☐ Axe
- ☐ Bead breaker
- ☐ Cable ties
- ☐ Chemiweld
- ☐ Cold chisel
- ☐ Dark glasses (for welding duties)
- ☐ Duct tape
- ☐ Electrical connectors

- ☐ Electrical wire
- ☐ Feeler gauges
- ☐ Fencing wire
- ☐ Grease
- ☐ Ground sheet
- ☐ Hammer
- ☐ Insulation tape
- ☐ Jack to suit increased weight & height of vehicle
- ☐ Jack plate
- ☐ Jumper leads
- ☐ Leather gloves
- ☐ Magnet
- ☐ Measuring tape
- ☐ Metal putty
- ☐ Multi grips
- ☐ Multimeter
- ☐ Nuts and bolts
- ☐ Overalls
- ☐ Pliers- flat
- ☐ Pliers – long nose
- ☐ Pliers – multi grip
- ☐ Radiator stop leak

- ☐ Rubber mallet
- ☐ Screwdriver – flat
- ☐ Screwdriver – Phillips head
- ☐ Screws
- ☐ Shifter
- ☐ Shovel
- ☐ Silastic
- ☐ Small mirror
- ☐ Socket set
- ☐ Soldering kit
- ☐ Spanners – open
- ☐ Spanners – ring
- ☐ Stanley knife
- ☐ Super glue
- ☐ Torch
- ☐ Tyre pressure gauge
- ☐ Tyre repair kit
- ☐ WD 40
- ☐ Welding rods
- ☐ Wire brush
- ☐ Wire cutters

recovery equipment

- [ ] Bow or bush saw
- [ ] Bridle
- [ ] Drag chain
- [ ] D shackles minimum rating 3.25 tonne
- [ ] Exhaust jack
- [ ] Fire extinguisher
- [ ] Gloves
- [ ] Ground sheet or tarp
- [ ] Jack and jacking plate
- [ ] Manual winch
- [ ] Sand tracks
- [ ] Spade
- [ ] Snatch block
- [ ] Snatch strap
- [ ] Tie down straps (ratchet style)
- [ ] Tree trunk protector
- [ ] Winch strap extension

camping equipment

- [ ] Air mattress (self-inflating)
- [ ] Axe
- [ ] Bag for soiled clothes
- [ ] Bucket (square or rectangular shape)
- [ ] Clothes line rope
- [ ] Camp chairs
- [ ] Clothes pegs
- [ ] Dust pan and brush
- [ ] First-aid kit
- [ ] Fluoro light
- [ ] Garbage bags
- [ ] Gas bottle
- [ ] Gas cooker
- [ ] Ground sheet
- [ ] Head torch
- [ ] Pillow/pillow case
- [ ] Rope
- [ ] Screen tent
- [ ] Sleeping bag
- [ ] Shower (portable or engine mounted)
- [ ] Swag
- [ ] Table
- [ ] Tent
- [ ] Tent pegs plus spare pegs

- [ ] Tent poles
- [ ] Tent rope
- [ ] Toilet seat
- [ ] Toilet or shower screen
- [ ] Torch batteries
- [ ] Torch globe (spare)

washing equipment

- [ ] Brush
- [ ] Clothes line
- [ ] Coins for washing machines
- [ ] Detergent (biodegradeable)
- [ ] Pegs
- [ ] Scourer
- [ ] Sponge
- [ ] Tea towels
- [ ] Wash up bucket (square or rectangular)
- [ ] Washing powder – clothes

cooking/eating equipment

- [ ] Aluminium foil
- [ ] Aluminium loaf tins
- [ ] Baking paper

- [ ] Basting brush
- [ ] BBQ grill/plate
- [ ] BBQ scraper
- [ ] Billy
- [ ] Billy stand and hooks
- [ ] Camp oven
- [ ] Camp oven lifter
- [ ] Camp toaster
- [ ] Can opener
- [ ] Carving knife
- [ ] Cereal/dessert bowl
- [ ] Cork screw
- [ ] Cutting board
- [ ] Dinner plates
- [ ] Drink bottles
- [ ] Egg flip
- [ ] Egg rings
- [ ] Egg whisk
- [ ] Fire lighters
- [ ] Forks
- [ ] Frypan
- [ ] Gas bottle

- [ ] Gas burner
- [ ] Gas lighter
- [ ] Gloves
- [ ] Grater
- [ ] Jaffle iron
- [ ] Matches
- [ ] Mugs
- [ ] Paper towels
- [ ] Plastic bags
- [ ] Plastic storage containers of various sizes (square or rectangular) with air tight lids
- [ ] Plastic wrap
- [ ] Saucepans
- [ ] Serrated edge knife
- [ ] Spoon
- [ ] Strainer/slotted spoon
- [ ] Steak knifes
- [ ] Teaspoons
- [ ] Thermos
- [ ] Tongs
- [ ] Vegetable peeler
- [ ] Water

- [ ] Water container (5 litres for easy use during meal preparation)
- [ ] Zip lock bags

personal gear

- [ ] Antiseptic cream/wash
- [ ] Comb
- [ ] Conditioner
- [ ] Cotton buds
- [ ] Deodorant
- [ ] Face washer
- [ ] First-aid kit and manual
- [ ] Fly net for the hat/head
- [ ] Hair brush
- [ ] Hat/Cap/Beanie
- [ ] Headache tablets
- [ ] Insect repellent
- [ ] Lip cream/balm
- [ ] Mirror
- [ ] Moistened towelettes
- [ ] Moisturiser
- [ ] Powder
- [ ] Prescription drugs

- [ ] Razor
- [ ] Shampoo
- [ ] Shave cream
- [ ] Soap
- [ ] Soap container
- [ ] Sunscreen
- [ ] Tinea powder/cream
- [ ] Tissues
- [ ] Toilet paper
- [ ] Toothbrush
- [ ] Toothpaste
- [ ] Towel

other/miscellaneous

- [ ] Binoculars
- [ ] Camera & spare batteries
- [ ] Camera flash
- [ ] Camera flash cards
- [ ] Camera manual
- [ ] Camera tripod
- [ ] Compass
- [ ] Contact numbers

- [ ] Credit cards
- [ ] Diary
- [ ] EPIRB/PLB
- [ ] GPS and batteries
- [ ] Health insurance cards
- [ ] Inverter
- [ ] Insurance papers
- [ ] Keys/spare keys
- [ ] Laptop and cables for down loading photos
- [ ] Maps
- [ ] Motoring and social club membership
- [ ] Pencils/pens/highlighters
- [ ] Permits
- [ ] Satellite telephone
- [ ] Wet weather gear
- [ ] Scissors
- [ ] Sewing kit
- [ ] Sunglasses
- [ ] Thongs
- [ ] Video camera and manual
- [ ] Wallet

Kimberley rock art, King Edward River, Western Australia

☐ UHF spare aerial

food

☐ BBQ sauce

☐ Bread

☐ Bread mix

☐ Canned fish

☐ Canned fruit

☐ Canned vegetables

☐ Casserole bases

☐ Cereal

☐ Chilli powder

☐ Cinnamon sugar

☐ Coffee

☐ Cordial

☐ Cornflour

☐ Curry powder

☐ Custard powder

☐ Dried fruit

☐ Eggs

☐ Fruit juices

☐ Honey

☐ Jam

☐ Long life cream

☐ Long life milk

☐ Margarine/butter

☐ Marinades

☐ Marshmallows

☐ Mayonnaise

☐ Milo

☐ Muesli bars

☐ Nibblies

☐ Noodles

☐ Cooking oil

☐ Packet pasta mixes

☐ Packet rice mixes

☐ Pasta

☐ Peanut butter

☐ Pepper

☐ Plain flour

☐ Rice

☐ Salad dressing

☐ Salt

☐ Savoury biscuits

☐ Self-raising flour

☐ Soft drinks

☐ Soy sauce

☐ Stock cubes

☐ Sugar

☐ Sweet biscuits

☐ Tea

☐ Tomato Sauce

☐ Vegemite

outback waterhole, Western Queensland

chapter 12

REFERENCES & RESOURCES

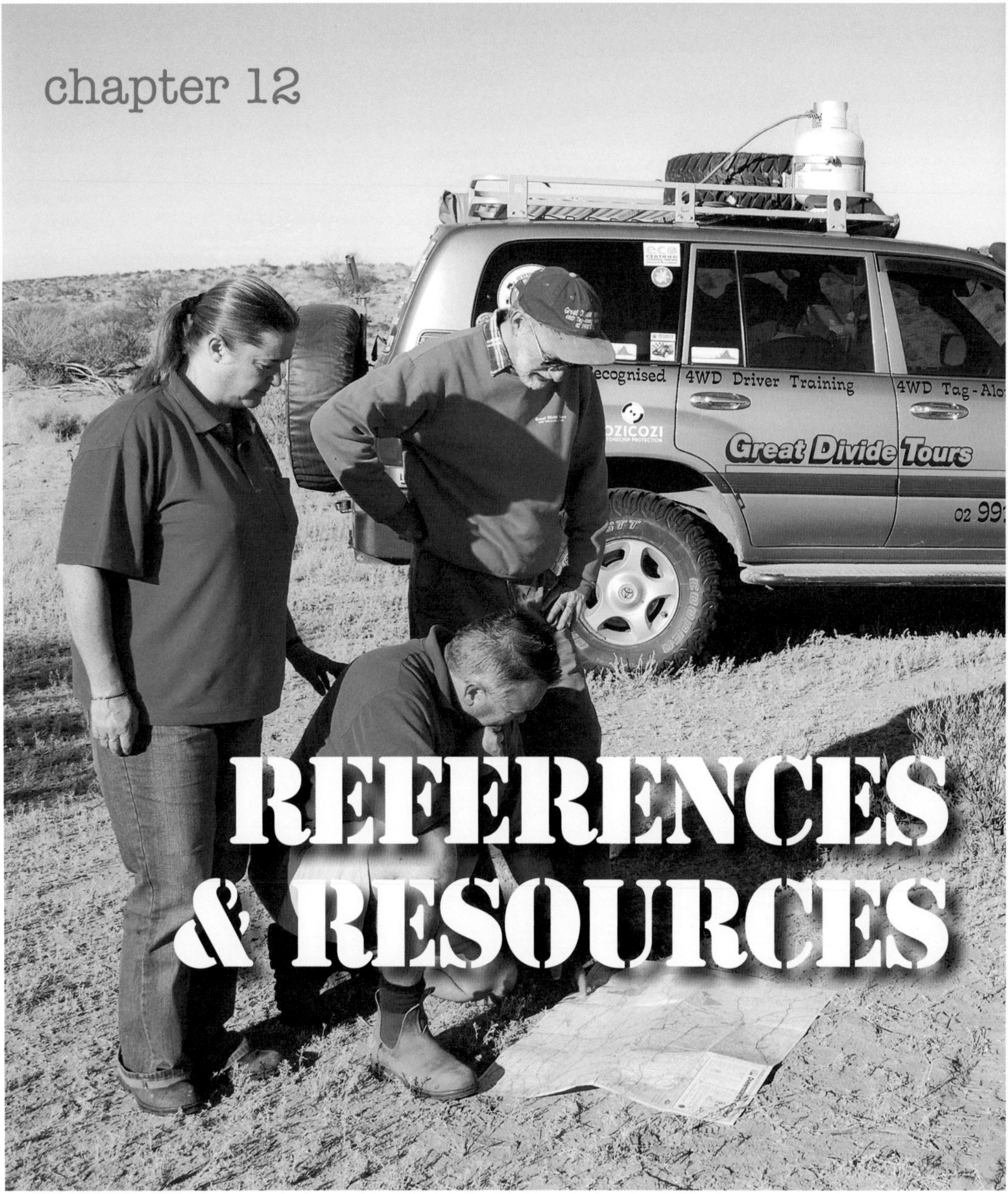

references & resources

Great Divide Tours
Tel: 02 9913 1395
Web: www.4wd.net.au

Boiling Billy Publications
Tel: 02 6494 2727
Web: www.boilingbilly.com.au

tourism sites

New South Wales
Tel: 132 077
Web: www.visitnsw.com

Northern Territory
Tel: 136 768
Web: www.travel.nt.com.au

Queensland
Tel: 138 833
Web: www.queenslandholidays.com.au

South Australia
Tel: 1300 764 227
Web: www.southaustralia.com

Tasmania
Tel: 1300 780 867
Web: www.discovertasmania.com.au

Victoria
Tel: 132 842
Web: www.visitvictoria.com

Western Australia
Tel: 1300 361 351
Web: www.westernaustralia.com.au

national parks

National
Australian Government Department of Environment,
Water, Heritage and the Arts
Tel: 02 6274 1111
Web: www.environment.gov.au/parks

New South Wales
National Parks & Wildlife
Tel: 1300 361 967
Web: www.nationalparks.nsw.gov.au

Northern Territory
Parks & Wildlife Commission of the Northern
Territory
Tel: 8999 4555
Web: www.nt.gov.au/nreta/parks

Queensland
Queensland Environment Protection Authority
Tel: 1300 130 372
Web: www.epa.qld.gov.au

South Australia
Department of Environment & Heritage
Tel: 08 8204 1910
Web: www.parks.sa.gov.au

Tasmania
Parks & Wildlife Service Tasmania
Tel: 1300 135 513
Web: www.parks.tas.gov.au

Victoria
Parks Vic
Tel: 131 963
Web: www.parkweb.vic.gov.au

Western Australia

Department of Environment & Conservation
Tel: 08 9219 8000
Web: www.dec.wa.gov.au

state motoring bodies

New South Wales
NRMA
Tel: 131 122
Web: www.mynrma.com.au

Northern Territory
AANT
Tel: 08 8981 3837
Web: www.aant.com.au

Queensland
RACQ
Tel: 131 905
Web: www.racq.com.au

South Australia
RAA
Tel: 08 8202 4600
Web: www.raa.net

Tasmania
RACT
Tel: 132 722
Web: www.ract.com.au

Victoria
RACV
Tel: 137 228
Web: www.racv.com.au

Western Australia

RAC
Tel: 131 703
Web: www.rac.com.au

road report/conditions

New South Wales
RTA Road and Traffic conditions
Tel: 132 701
Web: www.rta.nsw.gov.au

Northern Territory
NT Department of Construction and Infrastructure
Tel: 1800 246 199
Web: www.ntlis.nt.gov.au/roadreport

Queensland
RACQ/Transport and Main Roads Road Reporting
Tel: 1300 130 595
Web: www.racq.com.au/travel/Maps_and_
Directions/road_conditions

South Australia
Department of Transport, Energy and Infrastructure
Tel: 1300 361 033
Web: www.transport.sa.gov.au

Tasmania
Transport Tasmania
Tel: 1300 851 225
Web: www.transport.tas.gov.au

Victoria
VicRoads
Tel: 03 9854 2666
Web: www.vicroads.vic.gov.au

Western Australia
Main Roads Western Australia
Tel: 138 138
Web: www.mainroads.wa.gov.au

permits

Anne Beadell Highway
In South Australia permits are required from three separate bodies. Allow 4-6 weeks.

SA Department for Environment & Heritage
Camping permit required for Tallaringa Conservation Park and Mamungari (formerly Unnamed) Conservation Park, these are covered within a Desert Parks Pass otherwise obtain bush camping permit per vehicle/night.

PO Box 569, Ceduna SA 5690
Tel: 08 8625 3144. Fax: 08 8625 3123
Web: www.environment.sa.gov.au

Maralinga Tjarutja Land
Contact Dr Archie Barton
PO Box 435, Ceduna, SA 5690
Tel: 08 8625 2946. Fax: 08 8265 3076

Woomera Prohibited Area
Contact Wally Broom
PO Box 157, Woomera, SA 5720
Tel: 08 8674 3370. Fax: 08 8674 3308.

In Western Australia a permit is required to travel through Aboriginal reserves No 20396 and 25050. These are east of the Great Central Road and Laverton.

Department of Indigenous Affairs
Level 1, 197 St Georges Terrace, Perth
PO Box 7770, Cloister's Square, Perth WA 6850
Tel: 08 9235 8000 Fax: 08 9235 8088
Web: www.dia.wa.gov.au

Garig Gunak Barlu National Park
Permit applications are available from:

Parks and Wildlife Commission of the Northern Territory
Cobourg Peninsula Sanctuary and Marine Park Board
Permits Officer
PO Box 496, Palmerston NT 0831
Tel: 08 8999 4814 or 08 8999 4795
Web: www.nt.gov.au/nreta/parks/permits/cobourgpeninsula.html

Northern Land Council
45 Mitchell St, Darwin or GPO Box 1222, Darwin NT 0801
Tel: 08 8920 5100. Fax: 08 8945 2633
Web: www.nlc.org.au

Beagle Bay
A fee to enter the community is payable on arrival, this also allows entry to Beagle Bay Church. No camping.

Canning Stock Route
The Canning Stock Route is a public access easement which varies in width along the length of the route. Moving off the track for camping should be limited to less than two kilometres. The traditional owners of the land through which the stock route passes, the Martu people, are concerned about the protection of their native title rights and interests and their adjoining lands may not

be accessed without first obtaining a permit. The permit system to access the Canning Stock Route is administered by the Australian National Four Wheel Drive Council (ANFWDC) on behalf of the Martu people.

Australian National 4WD Council (ANFWDC)
Contact Canning Stock Route Manager
GPO Box 79, Canberra ACT 2601
Web: www.anfwdc.asn.au

Cape York
Alcohol restrictions are in place for remote Aboriginal communities of Cape York and northern Queensland. Restrictions differ from each community, contact below for details.

Aboriginal and Torres Strait Islander Partnerships
Alcohol Limits Information Line Tel: 1300 789 000
Web: www.atsip.qld.gov.au

Connie Sue Highway
Permit required to travel through Aboriginal reserve 40787.

Ngaayatjarra Land Council
PO Box 644, Alice Springs NT 0871
Tel: 08 8950 1711 Fax: 08 8953 1892
Or:
Department of Indigenous Affairs
Level 1, 197 St Georges Terrace, Perth
PO Box 7770, Cloister's Square, Perth WA 6850
Tel: 08 9235 8000. Fax: 08 9235 8088
Web: www.dia.wa.gov.au

East Arnhem Land – Nhulunbuy
There are several restrictions to access East Arnhem Land and Nhulunbuy. Firstly a travel permit is required to travel the Central Arnhem Road, these are available from the Northern Land Council, and on arrival into Nhulunbuy the first night's accommodation must have been pre-booked prior to arrival. To visit the recreational and camping areas on Gove Peninsula, general permits and in some instances special permits area required, these are available from the Dhimurru Aboriginal Corporation. Also please note that the East Arnhem region is a dry area and restrictions apply to drinking in public, a liquor permit system is applicable to the region.

General and Special Permits from:
Dhimurru Aboriginal Corporation
PO Box 1551, Nhulunbuy NT 0881
Tel: 08 8987 3992
Web: www.dhimurru.com.au

Travel Permit from:
Northern Land Council
5 Katherine Terrace, Katherine NT 0850
Tel: 08 8972 2799. Fax: 08 8972 2190
Web: www.nlc.org.au

Alcohol restrictions contact:
East Arnhem Land Tourist Association
Tel: 08 8987 2255
Web: www.ealta.org
Or:
Licensing Regulation and Alcohol Strategy, Nhulunbuy
Tel: 08 8987 0505

The 'Marble Bar' - Pilbara Region, Western Australia

Fraser Island

Permits are required to access and camp on Fraser Island, these are managed through the Queensland Department of Environment & Resource Management (DERM)

Department of Environment & Resource Management
GPO Box 2454, Brisbane Qld 4000
Phone: 1300 130 372
Web: www.epa.qld.gov.au/parks/iaparks/gds/

Permits are also available over the counter at the following outlets, but to guarantee a campsite in your selected area you are encouraged to book in advance.

Fraser Coast Visitor Information Centre
227 Maryborough Harvey Bay Road, Hervey Bay
Tel: 1800 811 728
Or:
Manta Ray Barges
60 Rainbow Beach Road, Rainbow Beach
Tel: 07 5486 3935

Gary Junction Road

Permit required for travel through Aboriginal lands in Western Australia.

Ngaayatjarra Land Council
PO Box 644, Alice Springs NT 0871
Tel: 08 8950 1711 Fax: 08 8953 1892
Or:
Department of Indigenous Affairs
Level 1, 197 St Georges Terrace, Perth
PO Box 7770, Cloister's Square, Perth WA 6850
Tel: 08 9235 8000 Fax: 08 9235 8088
Web: www.dia.wa.gov.au

Permit required for travel through Aboriginal lands in the Northern Territory.

Central Land Council
27 Stuart Highway, Alice Springs NT 0870
PO Box 3321, Alice Springs NT 0870
Tel: 08 8951 6211 Fax: 08 8953 4343
Web: www.clc.org.au

Great Central Road

Permit required for travel through Aboriginal lands in Western Australia.

Department of Indigenous Affairs
Level 1, 197 St Georges Terrace, Perth
PO Box 7770, Cloister's Square, Perth WA 6850
Tel: 08 9235 8000 Fax: 08 9235 8088
Web: www.dia.wa.gov.au

Permit required to travel between Kata Tjuta (The Olgas) and NT/WA border (also known as Tjukaruru Road).

Central Land Council
27 Stuart Highway, Alice Springs NT 0870
PO Box 3321, Alice Springs NT 0870
Tel: 08 8951 6211. Fax: 08 8953 4343
Web: www.clc.org.au

Gunbarrel Highway

A permit is not required to travel the Gunbarrel Highway, however a permit is required to travel along the Heather Highway; the main access route from the Great Central Road to the Gunbarrel Highway.

Department of Indigenous Affairs

Level 1, 197 St Georges Terrace, Perth
PO Box 7770, Cloister's Square, Perth WA 6850
Tel: 08 9235 8000 Fax: 08 9235 8088
Web: www.dia.wa.gov.au

Innamincka Regional Reserve

Entry fee and camping fee applies, alternatively
reserve is covered in Desert Parks Pass.

SA Department for Environment & Heritage Desert Parks Hotline

Tel: 1800 816 078
Web: www.parks.sa.gov.au
Or:

Innamincka Regional Reserve Park Headquarters

Tel: 08 8675 9909. Fax: 08 8675 9912

Kalumburu

Two permits required.

Entry permit.

Department of Indigenous Affairs

Level 1, 197 St Georges Terrace, Perth
PO Box 7770, Cloister's Square, Perth WA 6850
Tel: 08 9235 8000. Fax: 08 9235 8088
Web: www.dia.wa.gov.au

Recreational permit, fee applies.

Kalumburu Aboriginal Corporation

PMB 10, Via Wyndham WA 6740
Tel: 08 9161 4300 or 08 9332 7044. Fax: 08 9161 4331
This permit is also available by visiting the
Kalumburu Aboriginal Corporation office in
Kalumburu on arrival.

Simpson Desert

Mereenie Loop Road

Permit required for travel between Kings Canyon and Hermannsburg. Permits are available on day of travel only, for a small fee from the following:

Alice Springs Tourist Office
Tel: 1800 645 199 or 08 8952 5800

Glen Helen Resort
Tel: 08 8956 7489

Kings Canyon Resort
Tel: 08 8956 7442

Ntaria Supermarket, Hermannsburg
Tel: 08 8956 7480

Northern Simpson Desert

A permit and fee is required to access the Hay River Batton Hill Area.

Direct 4WD Awareness
Tel: 08 8952 3359 or 0408 485 641
Web: www.direct4wd.com.au/tours/hay_access.htm

Old/Abandoned Gunbarrel Highway

A permit is required to travel the Old/Abandoned Gunbarrel Highway. This section is from the junction of the Gunbarrel Highway and the Heather Highway, east to Warakurna via Jackie Junction. Restrictions apply to the number of vehicles in the convoy and specified safety equipment must be carried. Note: Issue of a permit cannot be guaranteed.

Ngaayatjarra Land Council
PO Box 644, Alice Springs NT 0871
Tel: 08 8950 1711 Fax: 08 8953 1892

Sandy Blight Junction Road

Permit required to travel through Aboriginal lands in the Northern Territory.

Central Land Council
27 Stuart Highway, Alice Springs NT 0870
PO Box 3321, Alice Springs NT 0870
Tel: 08 8951 6211. Fax: 08 8953 4343
Web: www.clc.org.au

Permit required to travel through Aboriginal lands in Western Australia.

Ngaayatjarra Land Council
PO Box 644, Alice Springs NT 0871
Tel: 08 8950 1711 Fax: 08 8953 1892

Simpson Desert

Desert Parks Pass required.

SA Department for Environment & Heritage Desert Parks Hotline
Tel: 1800 816 078
Web: www.parks.sa.gov.au
Or:
SA Department for Environment & Heritage Outback Regional Office
9 Mackay Street, Port Augusta SA
Tel: 08 8648 5328

Surveyor General's Corner

Contact the traditional owners:

Wingellina
Tel: 08 8956 7704
Or:

Irrunytju Community
PMB 52
Wingellina via Alice Springs NT 0872
Tel: 08 8956 7566
Or:
Ngaayatjarra Land Council
PO Box 644, Alice Springs NT 0871
Tel: 08 8950 1711 Fax: 08 8953 1892

quarantine

Quarantine Domestic
Tel: 1800 084 881
Web: www.quarantinedomestic.gov.au

South Australia, New South Wales and Victorian fruit growing areas
Web: www.fruitfly.net.au

New South Wales and Victorian Fruit Fly Exclusion Zone and Greater Sunraysia Pest Free Area
Web: www.pestfreearea.com.au

South Australian Fruit Fly Exclusion Zone
Web: www.pir.sa.gov.au/planthealth/fruit_fly

Western Australia Quarantine
Web: www.agric.wa.gov.au – then follow links to
Quarantine WA

communications

VKS737 – The Australian HF Radio Network
Tel: 08 8287 6222
Web: www.vks737.on.net

Landwide Satellite Solutions,
satellite phone hire
Tel: 02 6426 3333
Web: www.landwide.com.au

epirb and plb details

Australian Maritime Safety Authority
Australian 405 Distress Beacon Register
Tel: 1800 406 406
Web: http://beacons.amsa.gov.au

GPSOz
Tel: 02 9999 2313
Web: www.gpsoz.com.au

other sites of interest

Bureau of Meterology
Web: www.bom.gov.au

Royal Flying Doctor Service
General Enquiries Tel: 02 8259 8101
Web: www.flyingdoctor.net

ExplorOz
Web: www.exploroz.com.au

INDEX

index

A

Aboriginal land 138
adventure vi, vii, 1, 4, 15, 31, 69, 70, 104, 135, 190, 192
aerial 37, 80, 81
air bag 38, 75
air bed 53, 70, 71, 91, 95
air compressor 34, 35
air filter 64, 153, 155, 162
Alice Springs 1, 2, 3, 10, 128, 174, 186, 189, 190
all-wheel drive 24, 25
animals 15, 136
Arltunga 174
attractions 12
Australian 4WD RadioNetwork 81
auto electrician 58
auto/automatic 23, 26, 58, 160

B

battery 55, 58, 61, 63, 98, 99
Big Lap 1, 2, 70, 191
Birdsville Track 24, 32, 73, 76, 77, 136, 145
bore water 111
bread 120
breakdown 132, 166
Broken Hill 10, 128, 169, 170
Broome 10, 125, 190
budget ix, 75
bull bar 37, 38, 39, 66, 80
bull dust 154, 155, 174, 186
bumper bar 40
Bungle Bungle range 189
Bureau of Meteorology 3

C

Cairns 7, 10, 172
Cameron Corner 172
camp chair 101, 104
camp fire 14, 47, 89, 101, 115, 125, 138, 139, 142, 143
camp oven 100, 101, 120, 139
camp table 101

camper trailer ix, 5, 10, 25, 26, 28, 29, 40, 65, 69, 70, 73, 75, 76, 77, 146
camping equipment 25
campsite 3, 6, 12, 18, 26, 47, 63, 91, 104, 135, 136, 138, 139, 142, 149, 170
Canning Stock Route 24, 33, 38, 46, 58, 138, 148, 182, 183, 190, 225
canvas 28, 53, 70, 89, 90, 91, 95, 101
Cape Crawford 186
Cape York 14, 24, 33, 35, 77, 125, 145, 172, 173, 192, 225
caravan parks vi, 18, 106
caravan vi, vii, 2, 5, 14, 18, 24, 25, 26, 29, 30, 38, 40, 61, 65, 69, 77, 79, 106, 128, 129, 146
cargo barrier 53, 54
cash 53, 132
cattle 15, 39, 40, 81
CB radio 79
Chambers Pillar 3, 174
children ix, 10, 12, 14, 15, 18, 99, 104, 143
Chilli Beach 172
closed roads 12, 156
clothing 125, 126
corrugations 35, 38, 46, 52, 148, 149, 152, 182, 186
credit cards 132
cryovac 114

D

Dalhousie Springs 126, 135, 170
damper 120
Darwin 2, 125, 184, 186
deep cycle battery 58, 61, 63
Derby 190
desert 2, 3, 12, 15, 19, 24, 25, 29, 64, 91, 95, 110, 118, 129, 136, 138, 139, 149, 170, 172, 182, 225
destination 2, 14, 104, 114, 145, 190
detour 1, 2
Diamantina River 14, 172
diesel 23, 24, 25, 26, 46, 47, 49, 61, 99, 182
Dig Tree 172
driving lights 37, 62
dump point 106
dust 28, 43, 50, 53, 91, 125, 142, 152, 153, 154, 155, 156, 158, 174, 186, 189
DVD 14, 58, 76

E

EPIRB 79, 85

F

family vi, vii, ix, 4, 15, 18, 19, 25, 65, 69, 70, 71, 84, 86, 90, 100, 104
fees 4
fire extinguisher 47
fire pit 139
firewood 10, 50, 52, 94, 136, 139
first aid kit 64, 128
Fitzroy Crossing 190
Flinders Ranges 2, 169, 172
fluoro lights 63
fly net 126
food 15, 18, 19, 35, 55, 65, 96, 98, 100, 111, 115, 116, 118, 128, 129, 142, 158, 162, 166, 182
forum 4, 32, 73
four-wheel drive vi, vii, ix, 5, 10, 12, 18, 23, 24, 25, 26, 28, 29, 30, 31, 32, 33, 35, 37, 38, 41, 42, 43, 46, 47, 53, 54, 55, 58, 63, 64, 65, 66, 69, 71, 73, 76, 79, 80, 86, 90, 96, 98, 99, 110, 125, 128, 135, 145, 146, 148, 153, 154, 155, 156, 158, 159, 160, 162, 166, 169, 172, 174, 178, 182, 186,
Francois Peron National Park 178, 191
fridge 47, 55, 58, 64, 96, 98, 114, 115, 116, 118
fruit fly 109
fruit 109, 114, 115, 116
fuel consumption 46, 48, 53, 153
fuel 5, 26, 35, 46, 47, 48, 49, 53, 64, 94, 99, 100, 125, 153, 155, 162, 170, 172, 182, 189

G

gas lights 99
gas stove 47
gas 47, 63, 96, 99, 100
Gibb River Road 24, 29, 70, 76, 145, 148, 189
Globalstar 84
goal 1, 2, 7, 10
Google vi, vii, 4, 5, 81, 86
GPS 5, 79, 85, 86
Great Divide Tours 76, 225
grey nomad vi, 1, 2
ground clearance 37, 42
ground sheet 91

Gulf of Carpentaria 184, 185, 186
Gunbarrel Highway 152

H
Hamersley Range 190, 191
hat 99, 125, 126
HF radio 81, 158, 162
highway vi, 10, 14, 31, 32, 37, 52, 76, 148, 149,
    152, 155, 170, 172, 180, 186, 190,
HMAS Sydney 178
holiday ix, 2, 10, 18, 19, 23, 24, 32, 40, 53, 89,
    95, 104, 120, 125, 126, 128, 129, 148, 162
Hungerford 62, 63

I
information vii, ix, 3, 4, 5, 6, 7, 18, 19, 81, 85,
    86, 109, 158
insurance 39
internet vi, 4
inverter 55, 58, 61, 64
itinerary 1, 3, 6, 10, 135, 174, 192

J
jacking point/locations 41
jerry cans 26, 46, 47, 48, 49, 50

K
Kakadu 184, 186, 192
Kalbarri 178, 190, 191
kangaroos 38, 39
Karijini National Park 178, 180, 190, 191
Kimberley 1, 114, 125, 126, 184, 186, 187,
    189, 190, 192
Kununurra 114, 128, 189

L
Lake Eyre 2, 12
LED 99
lighting 55
long range fuel tank 46, 47, 49
Lost City 186
low range transfer case 25

M
magazines viii, 5, 32
maintenance 10, 26, 148

manual 23, 26, 66, 95
map vi, vii, 3, 4, 5, 15, 79, 85, 86, 109
mattress 95, 96
meat 100, 114, 115, 120
medicines 128
menu 100, 111, 114, 115
milk 116, 118
Millstream Chichester National Park 180, 191
mobile phone 61, 84, 85
modifications 24
money 23, 30, 47, 58, 64, 69, 73, 75, 84, 89,
    98, 104, 132
mosquitoes 95, 129
motorhome 26, 30, 106
mulga 101, 136, 139

N
national parks 18, 19
Ningaloo 178, 191

O
oil 10, 35, 38, 64, 118, 149, 162
Old Ghan 12, 170, 174
Old Telegraph Road 35
Oodnadatta Track 2, 10, 24, 29, 32, 77, 110,
    145, 148, 152, 170, 174
outback roads 12, 26, 38, 46, 50, 76, 146,
    158,159, 160
OZTENT 90, 91

P
packing 2, 14, 53, 94, 100, 115, 196
permit 5, 6, 7, 135, 170, 180, 182, 184
petrol 23, 24, 25, 26, 46, 47, 48, 49, 63, 182
pets 18, 19
photo/photography 2, 12, 15
Pilbara 126
planning vi, ix, 1, 2, 3, 4, 6, 7, 10, 12, 14. 15, 19,
    54, 70, 71, 76, 81, 100, 169
Port Augusta 14, 128, 170,
power outlet 55, 63, 98, 99
power 25, 49, 55, 58, 61, 63, 80, 98, 99, 153, 160
preparation vii, 55, 91, 118
prescription 128
priority 7, 10, 12, 70
problems 18, 29, 33, 50, 73

Q
quarantine 109, 114

R
rear bar 40, 41, 43
recovery gear 54, 64, 65, 66
recovery point 41, 66
Red Centre 1, 2, 135, 174, 175
reliable 24, 58, 81, 111, 182
repairs 52, 98
rest day 1, 7, 10, 14
retired ix, 1, 7, 190
RFDS 81, 128, 158
rock sliders 41, 42
roof rack 23, 33, 47, 48, 49, 50, 52, 53, 80, 90,
    91, 94, 128, 149, 182
rubbish 138, 142

S
sand 14, 24, 26, 29, 33, 35, 43, 46, 48, 49, 64,
    66, 70, 75, 76, 77, 91, 104, 110, 126, 135, 136,
    138, 139, 142, 154, 172, 178, 182, 191
sandflies 129, 132
satellite telephone 61, 64, 79, 81, 84, 85, 86,
    158, 162, 166
scenic 12, 18, 19, 94, 170, 172, 180, 189, 190, 192
sheep 15, 39, 40, 81
shock absorbers 35, 37, 38, 76, 149, 152, 162, 182
shower units 63
side steps 41, 42
sightseeing 12
Simpson Desert vi, 14, 24, 29, 30, 33, 46, 48,
    111, 125, 126, 135, 170, 171, 218, 225
sleeping bag 50, 53, 69, 95 96
solar 61
Southern Cross Canvas 89, 90
spare parts 38, 55, 64, 162
spare tyre 33, 43, 50, 75, 94, 142
speed 12, 31, 32, 33, 35, 39, 54, 85, 142, 145,
    146, 148, 149, 152, 154, 155, 158, 159, 160,
    162, 182
split rims 34
SPOT 86
springs 35, 37, 38, 76
storage system 53, 54, 55, 64
storage 48, 49, 50, 52, 53, 54, 55, 64, 70, 96,
    110, 111, 116, 118, 128

Strzelecki Track 145, 172
Stuart Highway vi, 14, 170, 186, 190
sunglasses 126
suspension 35, 37, 38, 39, 41, 75, 76, 145, 182
swag 26, 28, 46, 62, 63, 94, 95, 96

T
Tanami Track 145, 184, 189, 190
Teflon 100
Telstra 84
tent pegs 91
tent 10, 14, 18, 26, 28, 29, 50, 52, 53, 63, 64,
    69, 70, 73, 75, 89, 90, 91, 94, 95, 96, 99, 104,
    138, 166
Tiboobura 172
time frame 2, 7, 12, 65
toilet 94, 104, 106, 128, 138
Top End 91, 95, 125, 156
torch 99
torsion bar 37
touring vehicle vi, 24
tourist information centre 5
tow ball 66, 75
tow hitch 75
Toyota Landcruiser 23, 24
Tropic of Capricorn 2, 3, 125, 156
two-way radio 79, 81, 84
tyre plug 34
tyre pressure 32, 33, 46, 136, 155, 172
tyre repair 33, 34, 35

U
UHF radio 37, 58, 79, 80, 81, 84, 86, 153, 159
Uluru 2, 170, 178, 186
unsealed 3, 12, 25, 33, 37, 48, 69, 70, 145,
    146, 148, 152, 153, 154, 155, 156, 162

V
vegetables 100, 115, 120
vehicle jack 55
Vic Widman vii, 225
VKS737 81

W
walk 10, 12, 65, 73, 90, 126, 166, 180, 186, 191
water containers 110, 111
water storage 111

water 10, 35, 49, 63, 64, 65, 85, 91, 96, 109,
    110, 111, 118, 125, 128, 129, 138, 139, 145,
    158, 159, 160, 162, 166, 172, 182
weather 2, 3, 4, 10, 12, 14, 28, 29, 73, 76, 81,
    91, 94, 95, 156, 158
websites 4, 6, 19, 32, 61, 106
wheel carrier 43, 46
wildlife 10, 18, 40, 95, 138
William Creek 2, 12
winch 37, 58, 66, 76
wind drag 53, 94
wiring 58, 61, 98
woollen blanket 96

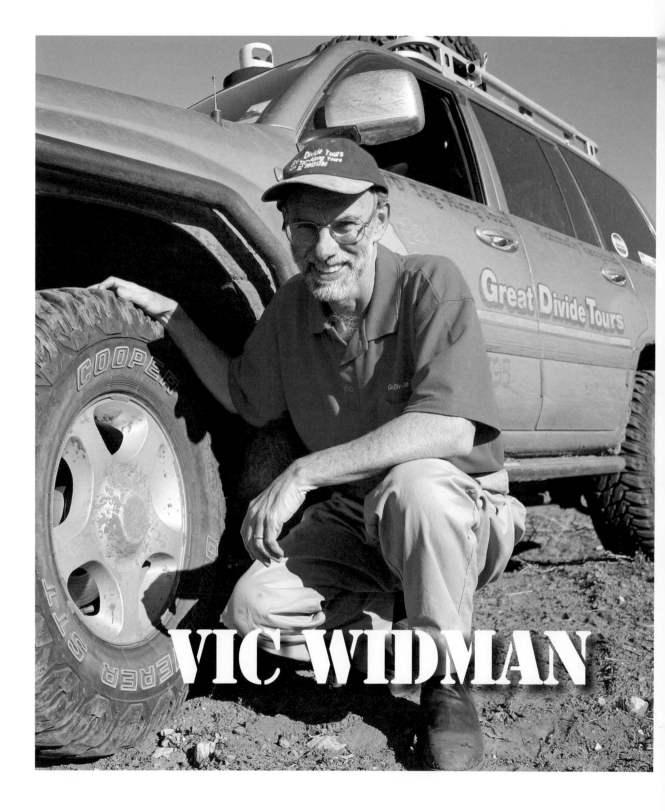

VIC WIDMAN

about the author

Vic started travelling the outback in 1978 and his first big trip was up Cape York in 1981 in a Subaru 4WD! Since then it's fair to say he has driven almost every road and track in Australia. He started freelance writing for numerous travel and four-wheel drive publications in 1985 and in 1990 he formed his company Great Divide Tours which has been leading four-wheel drive tag-along tours all over Australia since that time. Vic was also in the 4WD club scene during the 1980's being the President and 4WD instructor for various clubs in the Sydney Region. In 1992 he opened up what is one of the country's best 4WD training centres and in 2003 expanded this onto a magnificent 240 acre property near Braidwood in NSW. Vic is responsible for training in excess of 20,000 people in the art of four-wheel driving.

Vic penned the first edition of Travelling the Outback in 1999 and followed this up with the CSIRO publication, 4WD Driving Skills, based on his vast knowledge of four-wheel driving. He joined Overlander Magazine as a major contributor and columnist in 2004 and has been part of the Four Wheel Drive of the Year judging panel since 2005. His exploration of Australia has seen him cross the Simpson Desert over eighteen times, lead two hugely successful double crossings of the continent by four-wheel drive, explore the remotest regions of Australia including the Canning Stock Route and the vastness of the West Australian deserts and has now even spread his exploration internationally with four-wheel drive tours in New Zealand.

Travelling the Outback is a compilation of over 32 years of outback travel by, what Vic affectionately calls, a city bloke who loves the outback. He dedicated the first edition of this book to his father Jack Widman who also loved to travel and he again dedicates this book to his father who passed away in 2001.

To find out more about Vic and his Great Divide Tours visit **www.4wd.net.au**

boiling billy

Vic Widman's Travelling the Outback is just one of a growing series of outdoor guides from Boiling Billy.

camping guides

Expanded, updated and now in full colour the new editions of the bestselling range of camping guides from Boiling Billy detail hundreds of campsites in national parks, state parks, state forests, foreshore reserves and scenic reserves throughout the states. Accurate access information – most sites have GPS coordinates – to all parks, forests and reserves where you can camp, as well as comprehensive listings of facilities and activities available. Each guide is illustrated with full colour photography throughout and includes detail and regional maps plus a full state road atlas.

9781921203688 • **Camping Guide to New South Wales** • $29.95
9781921203978 • **Camping Guide to the Northern Territory** •$24.95
9781921606151 • **Camping Guide to Queensland** • $29.95 • late 2010
9781921203985 • **Camping Guide to South Australia** • $29.95
9781921606144 • **Camping Guide to Tasmania** • $24.95
9781921203671 • **Camping Guide to Victoria** • $29.95
9781921606168 • **Camping Guide to Western Australia** •$29.95 • late 2010
9781921606304 • **Camping and Caravanning Guide to the Murray River** • $29.95

guides for aussie bush travellers

If you're going bush, however you're going bush, there's a guide from Boiling Billy you'll want to take along. These new guides are illustrated with full colour photography and packed full of helpful hints, tried and tested tips and – in one case – delicious, easy-to-make meal ideas.

9781921203930 • Australian Bush Cooking • $34.95

9781921203947 • Caravan, Campervan & Motorhome Touring Handbook • $34.95 • late 2010

9781921606175 • Robert Pepper's 4WD Handbook • $34.95

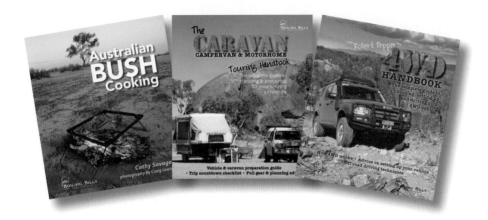

4WD treks close to sydney

Explore the best 4WD day and weekend destinations around Sydney. This completely revised and expanded 5th edition features twenty of the best 4WD treks within a few short hours drive of Sydney. You'll discover some of Greater Sydney's best 4WD destinations with this easy to follow route noted guide. Route directions read in forward and reverse as well as featuring both GPS Lat/Long and UTM Grid References. 4WD Treks Close To Sydney is the first in a completely new look series of 4WD trek and touring guides from Boiling Billy.

9781921606137 • $29.95

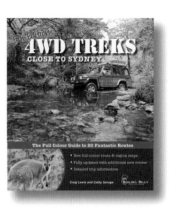